TRIUMPH AND DISASTER

The Autobiography of a Naval Officer

by

COMMANDER V.C.F. CLARK DSC* RN

If you can meet with Triumph and Disaster
And treat those two imposters just the same; . . .

RUDYARD KIPLING

PARAPRESS LTD
Tunbridge Wells

In the same series:

Dual Allegiance – From the Punjab to the Jordan, by Monty Green
Keep Your Head Down – Falklands Notes, by Cmdr. Bernie Bruen MBE DSC
Let Go Aft – The Indiscretions of a Salthorse, by Cmdr. G. De Chair DSC★
The Perilous Road to Rome Via Tunis, by Edward Grace MC
Wren's Eye View – The Adventures of a Visual Signaller, by Stephanie Batstone
Letters from the Front – WWI Correspondence of Lt B. Lawrence,
   by Ian Fletcher, Grenadier Guards 1916-17

© Victor Clark 1994
ISBN 1-898594-08-2

First published in the UK by
PARAPRESS LTD
12 Dene Way
Speldhurst
Tunbridge Wells
Kent TN3 0NX

A catalogue record for this book is available from the British Library

Printed in Great Britain by
The Ipswich Book Co. Ltd.
Ipswich, Suffolk

Foreword

This is an autobiography, starting at my birth – though I do not remember it! – and ending with the time of my marriage.

After that, compared with the adventurous days of bachelordom, my life, though very happy, was of private rather than general interest. The following narration, therefore, is confined to the days before I was (to the surprise of all my friends), 'sunk by a permanent wave'!

Contents

Chapter 1

My arrival in this world was hardly encouraging, my mother, on first sighting me, exclaiming, 'Oh, Doctor, is that mine?'

The doctor endeavoured to comfort her by declaring, 'Mrs Clark, he's a little beauty!' My brother had arrived thirteen months earlier, as bald as a coot and with brown eyes, contrasting with my shock of black hair and blue eyes. I cannot date my early recollections but I distinctly remember riding at one end of a pram with my brother at the other end. My mother said I was never happier than when sitting in a self-imposed mess, beaming with pleasure, caused perhaps by the accompanying warmth.

Born at Dover, where my father was Curate at the church of St James, I am on record as having exclaimed during one of his Easter sermons in the well decorated pulpit, 'What's my Daddy doing in the flower pot?' Frequent paddling in the sea from early months may have implanted in me the love of that element which pervaded the whole of my subsequent life.

When I was two years old the family moved to Bromley-by-Bow in the slums of London, my father being a Londoner born and bred and a lover of the irrepressible Cockney, and in these poor surroundings my brother and I were brought up for the next sixteen years. My father was now a Rector, and, living in a three-storey rectory with a sizeable walled-in garden and a nursery on the top floor, we were to a great extent shielded from the seamy side of things and enjoyed a very happy home life with a governess to look after us and such domestic help as a poor parson could afford. The pets which were always part of the family included, somewhat inadvisedly during the 1914-18 War, a dachshund, and not infrequently the gate would open for a couple of grubby-faced urchins to poke their noses in and call out, 'Come 'ere yer little

Jarman and let's make yer into sausages!' – and scamper off before they could be caught.

My mother was involved in a certain amount of parish work, such as mothers' meetings and Sunday school, and with a lovely voice herself she trained a women's choir which entered every year for the competition at the People's Palace, always to win the second place, never the first. But she never neglected her family duties, and amongst my happiest recollections are the daily readings in front of the fire before bed time of interesting or exciting stories such as 'Froggy's Little Brother' (to the accompaniment of much snivelling!), or tales of hero Raxworthy and villain Carr, from the early editions of *The Scout*.

Despite the sordid neighbourhood, we had a happy childhood, pretty self-contained but in touch with local clergy and doctors' families, and we enjoyed walks to Victoria Park and elsewhere. Every summer my father took duty in some country parish – perhaps in East Anglia, Hampshire, Berkshire or Sussex – and one year at Goathland on the Yorkshire moors, where, at age eight, I met my first sweetheart, to whom I remained devoted for two years. Her immediate successor was the daughter of a village schoolmaster. He fascinated us with his periodical beheading of a chicken on the front doorstep, as we watched the truncated body career around the school yard before collapsing.

In the Spring we usually stayed with our governess in Selborne, so we grew up with a love of the countryside. We were sent to Selborne, too, in order to avoid the fairly frequent Zeppelin raids on London. When we were at home during a raid, the rectory basement became a crowded shelter for parishioners, whose fears were calmed by hearty hymn singing, led by my mother. One holiday was spent at Hindhead in a house with extensive grounds, containing a cottage occupied by an elderly maiden lady. One day I happened to look through her window when she was having her bath, and of course called out to my brother Gordon to come and have a look.

'Go away, you naughty little boys!' cried the embarrassed old lady. Reluctantly, we did. The next day saw us calling on her with a bunch of flowers and my mother's apologies!

A regrettable memory of this period is of the occasion when my parents both had to go away for a day or two, leaving Aunt Millie (an honorary 'aunt') in charge of us. She wore spectacles on a spotty face, and was bossy and very unpopular with us. One day we pushed her up against the three-foot-high fire guard in the nursery, and whilst Gordon held her there I got a chair, stood on it and slapped her face hard. What happened on my mother's return can be guessed!

Gordon and I were great pals, although I do remember one occasion when we differed over a tin of Harrogate toffee. He had been sent upstairs to get it, and I intercepted him on the way down. A slight scar still remains on Gordon's left temple, from the wound I inflicted by grabbing the tin and hitting him with it! But in the main we got on well and had a lot of fun together.

My father always wore a top hat and walked everywhere at a rapid pace, usually leaving any companion trailing behind him, including my mother. Cars were a modern invention and mainly confined to the well-to-do. The costermonger with his donkey and cart was an everyday sight. My father had a great affection and respect for donkeys and used to raise his hat when he passed one, so he was in great regard with the costermongers, who imagined he was raising his hat to them. His cheery manner won him great popularity and he was held in such respect that on more than one occasion a during a riot (one of which was due to a perfectly harmless German shopkeeper) he was called in by the police to pacify the crowd.

They were days of desperate poverty in East London, and therefore of thieving. My mother warned her housekeeper never to let anyone in. One day she went to her jewel box and found it empty.

'Mrs Taylor,' she said, 'has anyone been up to my bedroom?'

Someone had. A man had called saying he had come to test the water tanks at the top of the house. When Mrs Taylor had offered to show him up, he had said, 'Oh, don't bother. I know this house well.' Stupidly she had let him go up, and he had helped himself.

Gordon and I were taught at home by a governess, up to the age of nine in my case, ten in his. 'Faggie', as the second one was called, Miss Fagge being her name, had a face like a cow, which she used to say was due to being weaned on cow's milk. Our governess taught us well and on going to a preparatory school we romped ahead of our contemporaries.

Our time at the first school ended abruptly in mid-term. In our weekly letter home, we mentioned that at the moment one of the two co-headmasters was gathering a large bunch of nettles with which to beat the bare bottoms of evildoers, and that the other had pinched me under the armpit and caused a swollen lump. A day or so later the two of us were unexpectedly summoned to the headmaster's drawing room, where the senior headmaster, whilst denying nothing, was furiously abusing my father for calling him to account for his cruelty. My father, cool as a cucumber, inspected my armpit, then told us to go and pack our bags and come home with him.

Our next school, South Lodge, Lowestoft, was a great success and we spent four happy years there before going on to public schools. The headmaster, the Rev. Richmond Phillips, was a severe-looking man with a beard which seemed to us to curl upwards when he was either very amused or angry. I only remember incurring his wrath once. On the last night of term I was having a pillow fight with a boy whose bed was by the window, when a blow propelled him reeling backwards and his backside sent the window tinkling to the pavement below. We both spent several hours down in the classroom learning some ten lines of Virgil before returning to our beds.

Academically, my particular aptitude was for mathematics. I was doing differential calculus at age twelve, and my maths master, T.J.E. Sewell, stayed with us during the summer holidays in order to coach me for a scholarship which I eventually obtained to Haileybury. Many a ride do I remember having in those traffic-free days on the handlebars of his Rudge Whitworth bike with its backpedalling brake.

One of the matrons at South Lodge, known as 'The Cat', was

4

bossy and unpopular. She kept a large stock of Gregory powder, a revolting cure for constipation, which she administered at times as a punishment for boys who displeased her. My brother was a recipient one day, and so angry that he threw it in her face. She reported him to 'The Beak' (the house master), and in the interests of discipline he made Gordon drink some, but afterwards she was reprimanded for prescribing such a punishment.

Our Sunday walks, collecting cornelians and agates, frequently took us along the beach in the direction of Kessingland, a coastal village where Rider Haggard had converted some old coastguard cottages into a lovely house, standing near the edge of the cliff. He was my favourite author, the first of his books to be read being *Nada the Lily*. I was so thrilled that I wrote him a letter telling him how much I had enjoyed it. I remember writing it in the Matron's room, for fear of being made fun of, and giving it to her to post. I got a postcard back which read:

Dear Victor Clark,

     I am so glad you enjoyed reading Nada the Lily. I have written lots more books and I hope you will read and enjoy them all just as much.

                               H. Rider Haggard

It was decent of him.

I spent one holiday staying with Captain Sewell in Rider Haggard's house, being coached in maths and Latin. It was a fascinating house, with the original etchings for his books framed and decorating the staircase and some of the rooms. One recollection still makes me blush. I got down to breakfast one morning before my host, and on the table was a bowl of rather lumpy dark brown sugar. Tempted beyond resistance, I was picking out the lumps with my finger when I heard a familiar nasal voice on the staircase say, 'And does it taste nice, little man?' I owe more to him than to anyone other than my parents, and he remained a close friend until his death some forty years later.

The Britten family lived near the school. Bobby Britten, Benjamin's brother, was a close friend, so we paid frequent visits to his home, getting to know his parents, his two sisters, Barbara and Beth (with whom I fell in undeclared love) and little Benjamin, who even at the age of about six showed promise of being a brilliant performer on the piano.

I enjoyed my years at Haileybury. I was never one of the 'bloods', but nobody loved the rare cross-country run or a game of rugger on a slushy ground more than I did. We did not regard life there as tough (do boys ever?), but it is less so now, and amongst the customs which have since been dropped – regrettably, to my mind – was the cold bath.

We used the bathroom twice a day: on rising in the morning, and after games, cleaning ourselves from top to toe at basins and footbaths, completing our ablutions with a compulsory plunge into a bath of running cold water, winter notwithstanding. Two prefects, lying in a nice hot bath, saw to it that we did. Prefects were allowed to cane. As victims we had to kneel on a chair, lean right over the top and grasp the back legs. This salutary correction can now only be administered by a master.

The fagging system was in use. Every prefect had a personal fag who looked after his cubicle. Additionally, at the cry 'Faggable!' everyone who had been less than a year at College, if he was not a personal fag, rushed at full speed to the caller. The last to arrive was normally given the job to do. The fagging system taught one respect for one's seniors and to do a job properly – or else! A system which encourages 'fighting, fagging, flogging' may be obsolescent (bearing in mind the exaggerated connotation of the word 'flogging'), but undoubtedly helps to mould a manly character.

House Prefect, and Captain of house swimming, were the peaks of my achievement at College, other than scholastically, and my House Master was, I think, rather surprised at my determination to enter the Navy; his own brilliant brother was on the ladder towards the highest rank in that Service. But my mind had been made up at age four, and despite discouragement from all and sundry it never changed. I remember him filling up my record form for the Navy examination. It was not by any means outstanding, and I distinctly recollect the sigh with which he asked me how I would like him to answer the final question: 'What hobbies or other interests has he?', to which I replied enthusiastically, 'Naval history and literature, Sir.'

In the event, it was that which caught the eye of the Admiral presiding at my interview and, after a fascinating quarter of an hour, it was that which resulted in my coming third in 'Interview and Record' out of two hundred candidates. The only two to beat me were 'bloods' from Wellington with terrific records, so I realised that my interview, revealing my knowledge of Naval history, had won the day for me.

I thought I would play a prank on my schoolmates on leaving Haileybury. I knew when the next term started and that the London contingent would leave Liverpool Street by the 3.10 train; so I decided to go up disguised as a navvy. For weeks beforehand I studied the navvy fashions in East London, where we were still living, and a day or two before the start of term I acquired the necessary clothes from a pawnbroker in Commercial Road, Poplar, and hid them in the Rectory boxroom. I was accompanying my mother in house-hunting at the time, my father having been appointed to a City church (St Stephen's, Walbrook) with no rectory, and on the vital day I was with her in Greenwich. What excuse I made to get away, I cannot remember, but I deserted my poor mother and returned home.

The sexton-cum-verger co-operated splendidly and I changed in the church boiler room, sending him out at the last minute to buy me some 'shag'. Then, as nonchalantly as I could in my navvy get-up, with a dirty face and hands, a false moustache purchased at Gamages, and a clay pipe in my mouth, I sauntered through my father's parish to the Underground station about a mile away, feeling extremely self-conscious. One draw of the shag nearly knocked me out!

Arriving at Liverpool Street Station, I sat for a time reading the racing news in the *Evening Standard*; then, when the boys had collected at the carriage doors, I bought a platform ticket and ambled down the platform and back. Regrettably, I did not have the courage to declare myself, but I wrote afterwards. On return, I did a quick change in the boiler room, and, respectable once more, I entered the house.

Chapter 2

On board the training ship *Erebus* at Devonport, we slept like
sardines in a tin, in hammocks slung beneath an uncorked steel
deck on which the breath of scores of snoring cadets condensed
and dripped on us as we slept. But the romance of my first few
nights on board ship outweighed such inconveniences, and I was
heard to heave a sigh in the night and murmur, 'This is heaven!',
which my fellow cadets never allowed me to forget. Whenever
anything particularly unpleasant occurred, someone would be
sure to say, 'Well, Clark, this is heaven!' In other respects, at least,
the first few days were more like hell, as we were chivvied and
chased mercilessly by the Staff and senior cadets whipping us into
shape.

It was in the *Erebus* that I first acquired my love of sailing,
mainly when crewing whalers or gigs for a fellow cadet in the
weekly sailing races in Plymouth Sound. At this period also, both
while still at Haileybury and after joining the Navy, when on
holiday or leave, I went to sea in Lowestoft fishing smacks as an
unpaid deckhand, always choosing one that had no engine. Skipper
Dale of the *Holkar*, a splendid burly character, usually took me,
regaling me with yarns of the 1914-18 War. Over the years I went
for six cruises of a week each, in all seasons from summer to mid-
winter, and once on Christmas Day. I encountered all weathers
from flat calm to gale, and incidentally I tasted fish which one
never sees on a slab ashore.

After a year in the training ship *Erebus*, I was appointed as a
midshipman to the battleship *Valiant* in the Mediterranean Fleet,
which at that time consisted of seven battleships, an aircraft
carrier, three or four heavy cruisers, a similar number of light
cruisers, twenty-seven destroyers and three or four submarines.

Valiant was a happy ship, and in her I learnt to sail well by crewing for one of her officers in the Fleet sailing regattas. By the time I had done my three months' destroyer training in H.M.S. *Wren*, I was an accomplished helmsman and was allowed to carry out in a whaler under sail, duties which were routinely done by a motor boat.

Whilst serving in the *Valiant*, I acquired a 500cc Sareola (nicknamed 'Sarah') in Nice. This was succeeded in the course of time by a New Imperial ('Rebecca') and two Nortons (both called 'Rachel'). 'Rebecca' was my first experience of a twist throttle, as opposed to an s-lever, and I shall never forget the hair-raising drive from Great Portland Street, down Oxford Street, Park Lane and through London to Bromley, whither my mother's house-hunting had eventually led, trying to control a motor cycle like an unbroken horse in the midst of the London traffic.

As a midshipman in the *Valiant*, and the *Warspite*, and subsequently in destroyers, I was allowed to take my bike on board during cruises. In the *Valiant*'s gunroom we had eight motor bikes, on which we did reliability trials over the Malta countryside. On one occasion I was stopped by a Maltese police-man, when driving the wrong way down a one-way street in Valetta. When he started questioning me and taking out his note-book, I let in the clutch and shot off round a nearby corner, hoping he had not had time to note my strange registration number, which was Belgian. But he had, and I was summoned before a Maltese magistrate, who merely shook hands with me, expressing the hope that it would not happen again – which was kind of him and made me feel rather ashamed.

Another brush with the police took place a couple of years later. I cannot remember what my alleged offence was, but I was detained in the police station at Sliema, despite my protests, for about two hours. I was so angry that I put in an official protest to my Captain. He supported me in forwarding it to the Rear Admiral (Destroyers), who in turn supported me in passing it on to the Commander-in-Chief. The latter, however, 'found it impossible to view Sub-lieutenant Clark's conduct other than with disapproval.'!

On a cruise to Jaffa during my midshipman days, I landed my bike, having got two days' leave, and covered over 400 miles through the Holy Land – Jaffa to Jerusalem, Bethlehem, Nazareth and Galilee. During a rainstorm which occurred whilst I was passing through Cana, my bike broke down, and I was pushing it uphill on the road to Nazareth when two young Arabs returning from work motioned to me to follow them. They took me to their home, put the bike in an out-house, then led me into the house, where I met their parents, an elderly couple reminding me of Abraham and Sarah, and a young woman with a baby whom I took to be the wife of one of them.

My wet clothes were taken to be dried, and I was given food and drink at a small table, sitting cross-legged on the floor. Hieroglyphics on the walls, which included a 12th-century sailing ship, enabled me to indicate that I was a sailor. They sent for a French nun from a local nunnery, after which conversation flowed fairly freely. I was bedded down for the night, and the young men asked me when I wished to go on, as they would push my bike to Nazareth. It was eight miles away! In the morning they were preparing to do this when I thought I would see if it would start, and with one kick it did.

My story was later told to the Bishop of Jerusalem, whose reported comment was, 'He was lucky not to have had his throat cut' – which made me think that he must be a bit out of touch with things.

As midshipmen we were expected to write home once a fortnight. One day, one of my messmates said, 'Oh Lord! I've got to write to that blessed mother of mine. What a bore!"

I said, half jokingly, 'Would you like me to write it for you, George?'

Like a shot he said, 'By Jove, would you?'

So I did, writing with my left hand, as from him, pleading damage to my right, and of course starting 'Dear Mummy' and ending 'Your loving son, George.'

In due course his mother wrote back enquiring, 'Who wrote that last letter? – it was much too clever for you.' Poor George!

11

'Anyway,' she continued, 'I enjoyed reading it and I am sending you a fruit cake which I want you to share with the writer of the letter.' It came, but I don't remember getting much of it!

George attended a levee at Buckingham Palace a few years later. The drill required everyone to gather at the top of the central staircase, roughly halfway along a very long corridor, for inspection of one's dress by a Palace official. George got fed up with waiting and started walking down the corridor. Before he had got more than a few paces, two figures in medieval dress on either side (presumably gentlemen-at-arms) crossed their halberds in front of him. Jumping back in surprise, George exclaimed in a loud voice, 'Good God! I thought they were stuffed!'

My next appointment was to HMS *Warspite*, as Senior Midshipman in the Gunroom. The Commander, 'Hookey' Walker, was a hero of the Zeebrugge raid in 1918, where he had lost an arm storming the mole; he wore a brass hook. During this appointment, four of us midshipmen were loaned to the aircraft carrier *Courageous*, sent to Jaffa to help to deal with the riots in Palestine in the autumn of 1929. We 'snotties' were landed and flown to Gaza aerodrome, where we were based for a few weeks. I recollect that the Wing Commander entertained a couple of sheiks, and was offered by one of them, Sheikh Freah, the choice of a camel or a white Arab steed. Unfortunately, Service rules forbade him to accept.

I had some flying in the back seat of a Fairey III F, and was passing over Jerusalem at the same time as my brother, Gordon, unknown to me, was patrolling the streets with fellow theological students from Oxford.

Gordon was at Wycliffe College, and on one occasion when I was visiting him there, I had been out to dine with a friend from another college. My brother had omitted to tell me that Wycliffe was locked up at about 11 o'clock at night, and I returned at midnight to find every door fastened and the place in complete darkness. I could only see one window open, a very small one, which I reached by climbing up a drainpipe. I hoisted myself in feet first, and fell inside, grabbing for something, anything, in the dark. Of all unfortunate things, I got hold of the lavatory chain! There followed a noise like Niagara Falls, which seemed to echo through the entire building in the silence of the night. I crept to my room hoping for the best, and fortunately there were no repercussions.

Courageous paid a visit to Cyprus, and we four snotties were treated by the Wardroom to a few days' break on Mount Troodos. I went on my motor bike, and broke down on the way. A passing Cypriot motor cyclist stopped to help me, replaced my sparking plug with a brand new one from his own kit, and firmly declined to accept payment. I spent the night in evil-looking company, and slept in a flea-ridden bed, but he himself could not have been kinder.

Warspite saw my only entry into the boxing world. I was keen for my Gunroom to enter for the Fleet boxing championships and felt I must put my own name down *pour encourager les autres*. In the first round I found myself up against one of my own junior midshipmen, and was beaten.

My heart-throb at this time was Winifred Shotter, with whom I had fallen madly in love over the footlights, when she was acting in *Rookery Nook* at the Aldwych. I was hoping to acquire an autographed photo, but on mentioning it to my messmates I was told that the whole of *Revenge*'s gunroom had written to her, one after the other, and after the sixteenth request she had replied, 'I do not send photographs, and I hope I shan't be bothered any more.'

I did not want to believe this of my lovely Winifred, so I concocted a letter saying how necessary it was for morale to be kept high by occasional favours from the fair sex, and that we were on the verge of fighting in Palestine, and asking, could she brighten up our lives with a photo? I signed the letter 'On behalf of Sixteen Saucy Sailors'. Eventually a lovely autographed photograph arrived which, as my messmates had been so sceptical and lacking in courage, I kept for myself. It adorned my cabin until I was sunk in the *Repulse* twelve years later.

As midshipmen, we had to keep a Journal. I enjoyed writing this up, and frequently included remarks on higher matters of

13

State. A bitter comment on the London Naval Conference resulted in a pencilled note in the margin from my Captain: 'You must learn not to criticise your superiors. Remember that they have forgotten more than you have ever learnt.' A piece of advice which I am afraid I have never learned!

I was on the station long enough to see Admiral Sir Howard Kelly take over the 1st Battle Squadron from his brother John, with whom he had been at loggerheads ever since (in their youth, so it was said) John had run off with Howard's sweetheart. Both were 'characters'. Howard was later in command on the China Station, and it was customary on Sundays, if the ship was in harbour, for wives and families to come on board for divine service on the quarterdeck. This was attended by the entire ship's company. The ship's Chaplain took the service, the Admiral reading the lesson at the lectern, on which would be the Bible open at the right place.

One Sunday, the story goes, on reaching the lectern the Admiral found it open at the wrong place, and showed great irritation and annoyance with the chaplain as he flicked over the pages trying to find the reading. After the service, one mother asked her little girl how she had enjoyed it, to which she replied: 'Oh, very much, Mummy, but wasn't God angry when he couldn't find the place!' This was told to the Admiral, whose comment was, 'And a very natural mistake for the child to make.'

John's sense of humour is illustrated by an incident during regatta practice, when he was Commander-in-Chief of the Home Fleet. After the Invergordon mutiny, measures for tautening up discipline included an order that no officer must leave his ship without headgear – uniform or plain clothes – otherwise he could not return a salute. John Kelly spotted a boat under oars about to pass his Flagship, coxed by the Rear Admiral (Destroyers) – without a cap. He proceeded to stand at the top of the gangway and salute as the boat passed. RA(D) was, of course, thoroughly embarrassed, he himself being unable to salute the C-in-C!

On my promotion to Sub Lieutenant, a year and three months of technical courses followed at Greenwich and Portsmouth. The

President of the Royal Naval College, Greenwich, was Admiral 'Ginger' Boyle, later Earl of Cork and Orrery, and a real fire-eater, the apostle of offensive action. It was he who had interviewed me for the Navy. He held a high opinion of the modern young Naval Officer, whose 'dash' he particularly admired (*pace* the police!) in driving from Greenwich to Waterloo Bridge in a normal nine minutes. But two young officers on my course with poor judgement as to practical jokes, were dismissed from the Service, after the local undertaker called at the Admiral's quarters to take his measurements for a coffin!

The probably apochryphal story goes, that on one occasion when ashore he saw a marine approaching, pushing a perambulator, and stopped him with: 'Now, I know your face, young man. Where have we served together?' To which the marine, saluting smartly, replied, 'I am your orderly, Sir, and this is your baby.'

Whilst doing the course at Greenwich and living in Bromley, not far away, I joined the riding class for officers and their families at the Royal Military Academy, Woolwich. The Instructor was an Army sergeant, whose invective spared nobody. On an occasion retailed to me by an Army friend, the class included an officer of noble rank who had a habit of picking his nose when his hands were not more usefully employed. The Sergeant Instructor noticed him doing this and bawled out, 'Mister So-and-So! Yer may be a Hearl or yer may be a Viss-count, but I won't have no hofficer a-pickin' of 'is nose in *my* ride.'

On completion of the courses, I was appointed to HMS *Anthony* in the Mediterranean, a destroyer commanded by Lt Comdr T.A. Hussey, who had been my Term Lieutenant in the *Erebus*. I joined *Anthony* at Gibraltar, a place which has always fascinated me with its historical associations, including the 'galleries' with their 18th-century guns overlooking the Spanish border. The combined Mediterranean and Home Fleets assembled there every year for exercises, then separated for ships to visit various continental ports. For these visits, officers from the Army garrison were taken on board to relieve their claustrophobic feelings, generated by being cooped up on the Rock.

On one occasion, a ball was given at the British Embassy at Lisbon, attended by officers in mess dress, including an Army officer from the Scottish regiment stationed at the time on the Rock. A Portuguese lady present saw him in his kilt, and went up to the British Ambassador in high dudgeon, saying that it was an absolute disgrace that at such an important function a British Naval Officer should turn up, not only in fancy dress, but disguised as a woman.

Lt Comdr Hussey was in due course relieved by Lt Comdr 'Bez' McCoy. I was a teetotaller at the time – as I was for my first eight years in the Navy – but I enjoyed the numerous lively parties we had on board as much as anyone, and my Captain almost invariably introduced me to his guests as 'our Sub who gets drunk on lime juice'. I was also sometimes introduced to his lady guests as 'our misogynist'. Of the origin of that misconception I am not sure, but it may have been when, as the youngest member of the Mess on a 'Saturday night at sea', I had to make a speech and propose the traditional toast of 'Sweethearts and Wives'. I quoted these lines:

> Oh, women's rum cattle to deal with,
> The first man found that to his cost,
> And I reckon it's all through a woman
> That the last man on earth will be lost.

It was while I was serving in the *Anthony* that an Admiralty Fleet Order came out announcing the possibility of a sail training ship being built for the Navy, and requiring officers to volunteer to serve in her. I was very keen, and my Captain was interested, but he was in the zone for promotion, so he went to see the Rear Admiral (Destroyers) to take advice. He came back saying that RA(D) had been to see the C-in-C (Admiral Chatfield) about it. Admiral Chatfield had expressed total opposition to the idea and said that he would take the view that any officer volunteering for it was merely out for a good time and not keen on his proper job. 'And', RA(D) added, 'I agree with him.' So my Captain did not send in his name: I did. Sadly, the scheme was killed when Chatfield became 1st Sea Lord.

The mutiny in the Home Fleet at Invergordon took place at about this time. At the first bit of rumour, the C-in-C Med took his fleet to sea, and kept it at sea until the mutiny at home was over.

I used to go riding at the Marsa race course with a fellow officer. The first time we went, my horse took me flying round at a racing speed and on reaching a certain point abreast the stables, without slowing down, turned sharp right and left me lying on the race course. Undeterred, we continued to ride regularly before breakfast.

The Med Fleet always went on a cruise during the hottest months but in 1932 the *Anthony* had the misfortune not only to remain in Malta, but to be at the bottom of a dry dock – the ultimate in heat. I always found it hard to cope with hot weather, and this I found impossible. I would sit at my desk, pouring with sweat and dropping off to sleep every few minutes. So I went to my Captain and asked for a transfer to the Home Fleet; appointment to the destroyer *Watchman* followed.

Chapter 3

Watchman's Captain was Commander 'Ginger' Lilley. He had a face like a piece of raw beef steak and his experience and efficiency as a destroyer captain was admitted by everyone to be unequalled. He did not get on well with his less experienced Captain (D). The flotilla was, on one occasion, proceeding throughout the night with divisions in line ahead, and station keeping had become very ragged by daylight when Captain (D) came on deck. Tart signals started flying in all directions, to the enjoyment of Ginger Lilley, who ensured that *Watchman*'s station keeping was faultless.

While this was going on, the Chief Yeoman of Signals on Captain (D)'s bridge, spotted *Watchman* flashing a signal to the rear ship in Captain (D)'s column. Evidently the assumption was, that in view of the direction in which the signal lantern was pointing it would not be seen by Captain (D). But it was, the two columns being at the time about as far apart as the distance between leading and end ships. The Chief Yeoman, in a stentorian voice which Captain (D) could not fail to hear, proceeded to spell out the signal as he read it:

'L...I...V...E...R... LIVER ...F...O...R... FOR
...B...R...E...A...K...F...A...S...T... BREAKFAST
...B...O...Y...S... BOYS.'

The flotilla was stopped and the Captain of the *Watchman* ordered to repair on board – in frock coat and sword. History does not record the conversation that took place when he did, but I imagine that Ginger Lilley's face was, if possible, redder than ever.

My two years in *Watchman* included two months on the Southern Irish Patrol – a fortnight at Cobh and a fortnight at Berehaven – under 'Bez' McCoy again as Captain, strangely enough. I was Sports Officer to the lively ship's company, and at Cobh organised a dance ashore. There was one girl, dressed in pink and exceptionally pretty, with whom I had dance after dance. A couple of days later we invited the dance band on board for a drink in the Wardroom and in the course of conversation with their leader I remarked that I had not enjoyed a dance so much for years. 'Yes,' he said, 'I could tell that from the number of dances you had with my fiancée!'

At Berehaven we anchored off Castletownbere, where my ship's company were keen for me to organise another dance ashore. When I mentioned this to the local Church of England padre, a wonderful man who always came on board visiting ships, he held up his hands in horror. 'Oh, you can't do that; Father O'Reilly (the Roman Catholic priest) would never allow it.'

'Well', I said, 'I'll call on him and try and arrange it.'

'Oh, don't you do that! He's a dangerous man. He'll do you harm.'

My right hand man as regards sport on the lower deck, a splendid fellow named Ritchie, was Roman Catholic, so I had a word with him and suggested that, if he was prepared to risk his skin and call on Father O'Reilly with me, we might get a favourable response, or at any rate avoid the forecasted violence. So we went, and after a very pleasant interview with this tough-looking priest came away with his complete blessing, his sole stipulation being that I provided a strong body of chuckers-out!

Another well known character was 'Auntie May', who ran a hotel at Glengariff. On anchoring there it was not long before we saw a dinghy being rowed out to the ship, heavily weighed down by the stern, where sat Auntie May. Her lightweight son was perched up in the bows with a pair of oars which found difficulty in reaching the water. She always provided drinks to the Wardroom officers free of charge, provided that they presented her with a ship's lifebuoy, beautifully painted and enamelled, of course, with the ship's name and crest. Her bar was festooned with them.

Mrs O'Shea was the owner of a little inn at Castletownbere and an enthusiastic friend of ours. She organised all kinds of matches between my ship's company and local teams, until the time came when there seemed to be nothing left to play. But Mrs O'Shea said, 'What about playing the kiddies at marbles in the Square?' We raised a team, and did.

Watchman's ship's company was a very sporting one and during a leave period in Devonport I was asked to arrange a charity football match against Plymouth Tramways. The only date that could be arranged was one on which there was an important rugger match, which was likely to affect the attendance at our football. Despite the fact that we had the advantage of free advertisement in all the Plymouth trams, I felt that additional measures should be taken.

At the Union Theatre there was a man with a performing seal. I went to see him and suggested that his seal might like to kick off at our match. He expressed his opinion that the seal would do the job perfectly well, but raised difficulties over transport and the cold, wet weather. I said that I would provide transport and blankets and, if he liked, an oilskin and sou' wester. But he pointed out that the seal was his livelihood and he could not risk its catching a chill and perhaps dying. So I had to think again.

There was a show on at the Theatre Royal in Plymouth, and I went along to see the Manager and asked if his leading lady could kick off at our match.

'Well,' he said, 'there are three leading ladies. Would you like to have a word with them in their dressing room?'

That in itself was an interesting experience, and I left having arranged for all three leading ladies to come. Despite the rival attraction, it was a successful day. The three ladies walked on to the field for the kick-off, the senior one sending the ball on its way.

In the course of conversation it transpired that one of the three – the youngest and prettiest – was keen on riding, so I arranged to take her out for a ride near Ivybridge on the edge of Dartmoor, travelling pillion there and back on my motor bike, in time for her evening show. All went well until it was time to come back, and my machine would not start! I am sure she thought it was a put-up job, and I got some dark looks! But after a while I did get it going, and a high-speed dash for Plymouth got her back in time.

I had another brief experience backstage after the War. A young friend of mine was acting in a play at the Criterion, Piccadilly, and invited me to look in. When I got there she said, 'Eartha Kitt is having a birthday celebration in the other room. I'm sure she'd be delighted for you to join us. I enjoyed a pleasant hour or so, and when I left Eartha flung her arms round me and gave me a hug and a kiss!

The only shore appointment I had prior to 1947 was a two-year spell (1935-37) training boys at Shotley, where I was one of the eight Divisional Officers, mine being Hawke Division. This was a life of ruthless competition which spurred the boys on to maximum effort, and all my energy went into insuring that Hawke Division were winners – subject to the conviction that my job in charge of 200 to 250 boys was to train that number, *not* to concentrate on a limited few with a view to winning competitions.

Nonetheless, in addition to winning more victories than was good for inter-divisional bonhommie as far as the other seven Divisional Officers were concerned, Hawke Division won the coveted Divisional Cup four terms running during my six terms of service there and again in the term in which I left. There was a prestigious obstacle cutter competition in which, after the term in which I joined, we were never beaten. I never allowed bad weather to interfere with Hawke Division's boatwork on the river, and the Division's efforts were at all times expected to conform with the motto which I had introduced for it: 'Hammer and Tongs, Hell for Leather and Blood for Supper', meaning *flat out*. The phrase 'Blood for Supper' was the most popular among the boys, and became their battle-cry!

Very often the weather was such that Divisional Officers preferred not to use their allocated boats, particularly in the early morning; but no boat was the preserve of any division and if not used was available for someone else, so at such times I made use of the extra boats for my crews. Sometimes the Commander took the decision and cancelled all boats. On one such occasion, I asked if I might take a whaler away with a good crew. The Commander said, 'All right, Nobby, but only if you go yourself.'

The crew rigged the boat for sailing alongside the pier, reefed well down, and off we went. The wind was against the tide, kicking up quite a rough sea, and each time we pitched into it sheets of spray came over the boat. We had to do a lot of bailing and we all got soaked but it was tremendously invigorating and I heard one small boy say to another, 'Isn't this absolutely grand? The sort of thing you read about in story books but never actually happens!' At that moment, I realised without a doubt that my rough-weather principles were justified.

Among the competitions that we won every year were those of the Inter-Mess and Inter-Divisional Boxing. The boys only had two weeks in which to learn to box amongst all the other activities. Boxing was a comparatively feeble exhibition for which I had no use, so my boys were taught to *fight*, and fight hard. From the beginning to the end of each competition I attended every event and made notes of the strong and weak points of each boy in the enemy teams. Then, when one of my boys was due to fight, I briefed him as to his opponent's weaknesses; e.g. 'no good at guarding his tummy', or 'wide open to a left hook', and so on. But always my final word was to go for him right from the start and keep on attacking him hard.

They won their fights, of course, against others who had been taught to 'box', and the finals invariably included at least one Hawke, if not two! The Physical and Recreational Training Officer complained bitterly that I was not producing boxers to represent Shotley in the Inter-Establishment Competition against *St Vincent*, so I told him to copy my methods and the evidence was that he would win.

To teach *helmsmanship* to two hundred boys in nine months was utterly impossible, and I gave personal attention to a small number who showed particular interest or talent. This was justified by the initiative shown by one of my trained boy coxwains during the War, as described later in the chapter on my Far East experiences.

Four of us – another Divisional Officer, the Doctor and the Captain's Secretary – spent one weekend sailing one of the whalers down the coast and up the Thames to Greenwich and back. It was one of the most exciting sails I have ever had. We got to Greenwich at about mid-day on the Sunday, to find everywhere as dead as the dodo, so set off pretty well straight away down river. We were off Southend at sunset, and throughout the night were beating up with a fresh breeze through the maze of shoals towards Harwich. It was dead low water off Southend. We had a good chart, a compass and leadline, and could pick out the light buoys, though there were plenty of unmarked shoals. In practice it amounted to sailing until we sighted breakers showing up white in the darkness, and avoiding them or making directional use of them. We had also brought an Aldis lamp for just such contingencies and managed to find the Spitway Gap by coasting down close to leeward of the Gunfleet breakers until we picked up the unlit buoy at the Gap with the lamp, and beat up through the channel. We got back to Shotley at 7am and reported to the Captain, who said, 'Now I suppose you are ready for bed!'

The following year I wanted to sail over to Holland. Our new Captain was not a sailing man like the first one, so I asked his Secretary, who had been an enthusiastic member of the previous crew, to make a good case for us. The request was turned down, and when I asked the Secretary about the Captain's reaction, he said, 'If you really want to know, he said you must be mad!'

The swimming bath in my time was boarded over during the winter, and served as a chapel. Even so it had a dual purpose, having a screened-off communion table at one end for the Church of England communicants, and at the other end for the Roman Catholics. Someone had had the ingenious idea of using for seating the old fashioned tram seats with swinging backs, that enabled one to face either way.

Each year at Shotley we had two Service guest nights, one for the Army at Colchester and one for the RAF at Martlesham. With the Army, the game was to get them climbing after dinner to the top of the mast on the quarterdeck; but the most memorable

23

occasion was when dining the RAF. After dinner, when they were engaged in playing snooker and billiard 'fives', I went out to the paddock, got the enormous grey mare, and rode her into the officers' quarters and to the billiard room. I had almost completed the circuit of the billiard table, when the mare stopped and refused every effort to propel her out of the door. At a warning cry from one of the guests, I looked round to see her tail rising. At the last moment – just in time – the Group Captain seized an enormous brass ashtray from the window sill and caught the mare's 'offering', after which she lowered her tail and carried me out of the room. It made the day for them!

There were two thousand trainees at Shotley, from almost every conceivable background, including the Gorbals in Glasgow. Needless to say, some of them found the discipline irksome and endeavoured to escape. The local police knew the top of every haystack within miles! On one occasion when I was Officer of the Day, one of the Petty Officer Instructors brought a boy along – a notorious 'skate' – reporting that some of the boys in his mess (dormitory) were plotting to escape that night, their plan being to wait until shortly before midnight and then, when the marine sentry's back was turned, slip out of their mess, break into the armoury where the ·22 rifles were kept, collect a package of ·22 ammunition which they had saved up surreptitiously from shooting practice and hidden in a hollow tree, and go to sea in a boat lying off the lower field.

I made the boy informer take me to the hollow tree and, sure enough, there was the packet of ammunition. The boy was then sent back to his mess and told to lie low, with a judicious mixture of praise and blood-curdling threats if he breathed another word to anyone. I mustered all Petty Officer Instructors on duty – about six in number – and explained the counter-action. The package was to be replaced in the tree, but full of empties instead of live ammunition. The duty sentry would be instructed to withdraw from that particular part of his beat from 11.30, at which time all Instructors were to report to me, each armed with a torch. We would then place ourselves around the tree in a ring, about ten yards from it, taking care not to obstruct the path which the boys were expected to take, which led through the wood and straight past the hollow tree. When I blew my whistle, all torches were to be flashed on the tree. Further action as required.

Well before the witching hour of midnight, we were in position. It was a pitch dark night. We heard the quarterdeck clock strike twelve. As it did so I heard a twig crackle, and straining my eyes I felt sure I could see a figure moving up to the tree. Yes, I was sure of it; close to the tree now. I blew my whistle and seven torches lit up the boy at the tree with his hand in the hollow. He dived down the bank, straight into the arms of the biggest Instructor in the establishment, known as 'The Shotley Terror'. He was escorted by the scruff of his neck to his mess, where we were confident of finding well known buddies of his. All was quiet except for snoring. Two blankets were whipped off by knowledgeable Instructors, to expose the occupants fully booted! They had been following at a short distance behind their leader and on hearing the whistle had turned and fled. I can still remember the look of hatred with which I was greeted on the quarterdeck!

Whilst at Shotley I had the opportunity of attending the only levee which Edward VIII held at Buckingham Palace. My father was Lord Mayor's Chaplain at the time, so we attended the levee together.

In the spring of 1936 the Swedish four-masted barque *Pommern* put into Ipswich with a cargo of coal, and I went on board. She was bound for her home port in the Baltic. I was told by her Chief Officer that she would be doing the same the following spring, which was when I was due to leave Shotley, so I made a tentative arrangement to join her for the passage to the Baltic when she next called. Sadly I was unable to do so: the Spithead Review in 1937 prevented it.

For the Review I had a temporary appointment as First Lieutenant of the destroyer *Wild Swan*. It was not a job I would have chosen, had I been a seer. She was based on Portsmouth and doing daily trips to sea running torpedoes, and was on two-thirds complement. For the Review the Admiralty called up reservists and pensioners, giving them to understand that they would go to Barracks, relieving the regular ratings at present in Barracks, who would make up the ships to full complement. On this understanding they all made arrangements for their wives to come and stay in Portsmouth too.

What actually happened was that they were drafted to the ships (certainly in my case) and saw little of their wives prior to, and nothing during, the Review. So I had the unenviable job of getting the ship, which was kept running until two days before the Review, into prime condition with a thoroughly tooth-sucking ship's company. On taking up our Review berth on D–2 Day, I decided I would have to give restricted leave, owing to the amount of work still to be done, a list of which was put on the ship's company notice board. At the bottom I put 'Two hand for the King and tons of elbow grease!'

That evening, passing the notice board when doing 9 o'clock rounds, I saw written in blue crayon against the last remark the word BULSHIT. I was furious, the more so as I realised I could never find the culprit; but sitting brooding angrily in the Wardroom some half hour later I had a mental picture of the notice, sent the Quartermaster to bring it down to me (which he did with a bit of a grin!) and wrote against the offending word 'This should be spelt with two Ls', signed it and had it replaced on the notice board. The following morning at Hands Fall In, every face had a grin on it and from then on everyone buckled-to with a will.

The Russians sent a ship to represent their country at the Review. British ships' companies man ship and, as the Royal Yacht passes, give three throaty, staccato 'Hurrahs'. Apparently the Russian cheer sounds rather like 'Boo-hoo', which occasioned the King to remark, 'They don't sound very complimentary, do they?'

After the Review, I was appointed to HMS *Warspite*, then refitting at Portsmouth and due to go out to the Mediterranean as Fleet Flagship.

Chapter 4

My new appointment presaged the only unhappy time in my career, owing to a clash of personalities with the Commander, though I made one or two very good friends among my brother Officers. These included Bob Ryder, who later won the VC at St Nazaire. He and I did a three-day tour, he on my pillion, from Villefranche up the Route Napoleon to the Swiss frontier and across to the little village of Termignon in the Alpes Maritimes. We had to approach our little pension between walls of snow and ice over six feet high.

By that time, we were getting sick of the garlic without which it seemed no Frenchman could produce a meal. So we said to the good lady in the pension in our best French, 'Il y a quelque chose que vous mettez dans toute la nourriture, que nous n'aimons pas. C'est comme un onion, mais ce n'est pas un onion. Qu'est-ce que c'est?' She went and fetched a complete garlic, which I sniffed and could smell nothing, and accordingly I signalled my doubts with a shake of the head.

'Ah, attendez!' she said, and fetching a knife from the kitchen she sliced it in half and held it up to my nose. There was no doubt about it! And wherever we stopped for a meal after that, we said, 'Pas d'ail!'

I carried my motorbike onboard until the War, both in battleships and destroyers, landing it at any place where the hinterland was of interest. For speed, my record run was probably when on holiday in Scotland with my parents, when I drove from Chatham to Strathyre, exactly 500 miles, stopping only for petrol and oil, in twelve and a half hours – an average of 40 mph, which was not bad in the mid-30s, when there were no such things as dual carriageways, and no by-passes to towns or villages. I remember being so

27

stiff as a result, that I lay in bed all the next day.

Despite my unpleasant relationship with the Commander of the *Warspite*, I found the social life of the Fleet Flagship pleasant. Amongst the friends whose hospitality I frequently enjoyed were the Lieutenant Governor of Malta and his charming and vivacious wife, Sir Harry and Lady Luke. We had a ball on board, to which I knew they would be invited as official guests, and I decided to invite privately a lady staying with them whose name I have forgotten, but we'll say it was Smith. In writing to invite her I was not sure whether to address her as Miss or Mrs, so I thought the best thing to do was to telephone their official residence, Casa Leone, and find out from the servant who answered.

Assuming that the brief words 'Casa Leone' were spoken by the servant, I said, 'Could you tell me whether there is a Miss or Mrs Smith staying at Casa Leone?' – to which I got the reply, 'Yes, I *am* Miss Smith.' Caught out completely, I silently and very gently replaced the 'phone on its hook. Miss Smith duly came to the ball as my guest, and during a dance said 'An extraordinary thing happened the other day . . .' – and out came the story!

I funked the truth: 'How strange!' I replied, 'but you know what Maltese telephones are like.' Who was bluffing whom I was never quite sure.

I left the *Warspite* without any tears in April 1938 to take up an appointment as First Lieutenant of HMS *Punjabi*, building in Scott's yard at Greenock, and obtained permission to drive home overland at my own expense. Taking the old *Knight of Malta* to Syracuse, I landed with a small Union Jack on my front mudguard, a White Ensign on the rear and two heavy suitcases on the carrier. I asked the Cook's man at Syracuse whether the flags would create trouble in Fascist Italy and he replied 'Oh no, but when you take in a couple of litres of petrol, they'll charge you for three!'

My route took me through Sicily, across the Straits of Messina to Reggio, up through Italy, over the Brenner Pass, through Austria, Germany and Belgium, crossing from Ostende to Dover and home to Bromley. It was an interesting eight-day drive, boiling hot in Southern Italy, and with heavy snow on the Brenner Pass. It was pretty rough going. The cobbled streets in Bruges nearly shook the guts out of both bike and rider, and by the time I got home the former was being held together with bits of string.

I was puzzled by the number of salutes I got as I drove through Italy, and discovered that I was thought to be a Fascist official of some sort, because I was wearing a black waterproof jacket and leggings and a black peaked cap. In Germany I kept passing huge pantechnicons on the *reichautobahns*. When I enquired about them from a young German motorcyclist whom I met and had a meal with in Weisbaden, he said, 'Oh don't you know? They are army vehicles; we expect to be in Czechoslovakia within a week.' I therefore sped towards the Belgian frontier, with my German friend accompanying me down the Rhine, pointing out places of interest and stopping from time to time to introduce me to the wines of the country. We kept in touch until the War.

My appointment in Scotland as First Lieutenant of the new destroyer HMS *Punjabi*, then building at Greenock, was likely to keep me ashore, and in the main detached from Naval life and company for a year or so, and I thought it was a good chance to grow a beard. The early weeks tended to be a bit embarrassing as, on my daily walk through the town to and from the ship, my scruffy chin invited giggles from the girls and jibes from the boys such as 'What! No razor?' For a short time I believe I was one of only two officers in the Navy with beards, the other one being a Captain with a rather prominent nose and a thick full beard and moustache which hid his entire face except for the brow (usually covered by his cap anyway), eyes and nose; his Admiral commented that he looked like a rat peeping out of a bunch of oakum.

Whilst I was in Greenock, I was determined to see as much of lovely Scotland as possible, so I bought a secondhand car, a sleek black SS Coupé, which my gunner almost purloined for me from a fellow in his cups. Its design was ahead of its contemporaries by years and people would stare at me as if I were Malcolm Campbell himself. It took me many hundreds of miles round Clydeside and the Highlands. Alas, my innate aversion to dealing with all things mechanical brought its inevitable retribution one day, when I drew up beside the road with a terrible loud clanking noise and found one of the pistons protruding through the side of the engine block. I sold her for £1 to a scrap metal dealer.

Punjabi's Captain, who joined her a year later, was Commander Trevor Lean, which I take pleasure in recording because of the affection with which we all regarded him. On one occasion, after a sweep of the northern waters with the Fleet, we anchored at Loch Ewe and I landed for a walk with our RNVR Sub-Lieutenant. It was well understood that we should not go out of sight of the ship, due to the possibility of an emergency call, but I regret to say that on this occasion we did, as a recall almost immediately after anchoring seemed so improbable. Returning from our walk, when we reached a certain point the mast should have been visible over the top of a nearby brae, but it was not, and to my dismay we saw *Punjabi* leaving harbour as we rounded the last point.

There had been a raider alarm and the Fleet was putting to sea again. *Tartar*, the last ship to leave the anchorage, picked us up, but for me there was the awful realisation that my ship was going to sea, hoping to meet and engage the enemy, minus her First Lieutenant and Gunnery Officer and one Officer of Quarters. Fortunately it proved to be a false alarm and, after what were for me two very uncomfortable days, ships were ordered to return to their bases – *Tartar* to Rosyth, *Punjabi* to Greenock. From Rosyth I made my way overland to Greenock and I shall never forget the guilty feelings with which I watched *Punjabi* approaching the pier. I reported on board to the Captain, expecting a thoroughly deserved imperial rocket with, perhaps, something worse to come, but to my astonishment he came towards me with outstretched hand saying, 'Number One [the soubriquet for First Lieutenant], my heart's been bleeding for you.' What a man! No wonder we all loved him.

After a time my Captain followed my example and grew a beard, as also did a number of the ship's company. Early in the War, whilst we were at Scapa Flow, the King paid a surprise visit to the Fleet and every destroyer was ordered to land two officers and a platoon of men for His Majesty's inspection. We piped all hands with beards to lay aft and had a look at them. Some of the beards were very wispy, but we managed to muster a full front rank of good beards and my Captain and I landed with them. The delay caused us to be the last to arrive and we were greeted with cheers (or jeers) by the rest already fallen in; but HM was quite impressed.

The regulations state that a man having a beard must request permission from the Captain before he shaves it off. When the first leave period of the War came along a good number of men went home with beards – and returned without them. They were therefore brought up as defaulters. The first one was asked why he had shaved without permission.

'Well, Sir, when I gets home my wife says to me, "What on earth's that you've got on yer face? Don't come near me until you've taken it off!", so what could I do, Sir?'

And all the rest said the same, and the Captain reluctantly bowed to petticoat government.

I was very popular with my relations and friends at the first Christmastide of the War, when rationing was severe. A workman on board *Punjabi* during refit in Glasgow had a brother who was a butcher. To solve the Christmas present problem, I gave him a list of addresses with the number in each family, and a suitably sized haggis was sent to them.

Winston Churchill, the First Lord of the Admiralty, also paid a visit to the Fleet and *Punjabi* was detailed to take him back from Scapa to Thurso. On the bridge he said to the Captain, 'Well, what sort of a war have you had?'

'We've had lots of anti-submarine work and some anti-aircraft,' the Captain replied. 'What we would like now is a good old-fashioned ship action.'

'We'll see what we can lay on for you', said Churchill – and within weeks we got exactly that at Narvik.

Chapter 5

The Second Battle of Narvik has been recounted many times elsewhere. Suffice it to say that *Punjabi* was on the destroyer screen escorting the *Warspite* up the Vestfjord and Ofotfjord. It was a glorious, sunny day, the water was blue and snow was on the hills. One could scarcely help reflecting, as we went into action, what a tragedy it was that such beauty should be the scene of carnage. No trouble was encountered from either submarine or aircraft: it was a ding-dong surface action.

Punjabi was unlucky in getting a shell in the boiler room fairly early in the action, which caused us to make thick, black smoke. This obviously presented a splendid target on which enemy fire control officers could direct their fire, and we stopped a packet. The vital transmitting station and wireless office were put out of action by a direct hit, so the guns had to go into local control. There was damage on the messdeck, with many casualties, and in the after compartment next to the magazine some flares were ignited. We had to go down and throw up the ammunition as quickly as possible under difficult and hazardous conditions. The Captain withdrew from the action for a short time to enable the situation to be got under control before returning to the fight. The German ships were all either sunk or driven ashore to be abandoned.

Punjabi, now looking like a pepperpot, had suffered more casualties than any other ship – thirteen killed and a number wounded. After temporary patching up alongside an oiler in Skelfjord, we returned to Scapa Flow with two German Officers from one of their transports, one a nasty-looking Nazi rat, the other a fine aristocratic-looking man of about sixty, who had, before the War, been Captain of the ocean-going liner *Bremen*. The flotilla Chaplain, whom we carried on board, was detailed to talk to them and get what information he could out of them. The most interesting remark was made by the ex-Captain of the *Bremen* who said, 'When this war is over, we hope you won't make another Versailles.' In other words, as a sailor he realised even in 1940 that Germany was bound to lose the War.

As a result of the battle, Their Lordships were pleased to award the DSO to the Captain and the DSC to me. I had the honour in due course of receiving it from the King himself.

On the fall of France we were ordered to St Nazaire to bring off British troops, with strict instructions not to bring off anyone else because of the risk of importing spies. As we waited in the dock at St Nazaire I noticed two pathetic figures, an elderly man and woman, on the dockside. I sent the Quartermaster to investigate and he reported that they were a Czech couple who had fled first to Austria, then to France, and had nothing except the tiny bundle they carried. My heart melted, and I sent him back to tell them to hide behind a railway truck. When the troops were embarked and the Captain gave the order to slip, I smuggled them on board quickly and down to one of the spare cabins, reporting to the Captain when we were at sea. He was not unsympathetic.

I told our RNVR Officer to look after them and make them comfortable, and he came up with a tiny photograph of the old lady saying, 'She sends you this and wants to know whether she can kiss you!' I suggested that he acted as proxy, but he declined, and I think she got her wish! They had to be turned over to the immigration authorities at Dover, and some months later a letter came from the old man to say that they had got good war work at Windsor, and beseeching God's blessing on me.

I could probably claim to be the only Naval officer who has been taken for a spy and also caught one – both while I was serving in *Punjabi*. During the War the only occasion apart from on official leave when we could legitimately leave the ship for more than about an hour was during boiler cleaning. Whilst this was being done at Rosyth, our RNVR Lieutenant (at the time Greville Howard) and I decided to go fishing. We stopped at a small hotel near a river where we were told we could fish, but first we sat down in the parlour for a drink. We then went over to the river bank. With only one rod between us, Greville was fishing and I was sitting at the top of the bank, when an Army officer came along and started chatting to me. Greville and I were both in plain clothes. After a minute or two our visitor said, 'You know, you two have been reported to me as spies. I'm the local Security Officer. The old girl at the inn rang me up and said, "There are two vairy suspeecious gentlemen here. Ye must come at once!"'

When he arrived, she had given him her evidence – all provided by Greville! He was wearing what I call an Austrian Tyrol hat, in which it was easy to stick flies, and which immediately aroused her suspicions. Then, she had heard him address me as 'Number One' (the normal way of addressing one's First Lieutenant), so surely I was an ace spy! Her fears were confirmed after we left by discovering in the ash tray, not Players Navy Cut or Wills Gold Flake, but the stub of a Weinberger, a rather exclusive brand favoured by Greville.

The Army officer was quickly satisfied as to our identity and, before going back to reassure the old girl, he begged us not to say anything about his visit, as of course she was only doing what he wanted, and I have no doubt that she got a pat on the back for her astuteness. But we could not resist a leg haul. Greville was an expert linguist, including in German, so when on our return to the inn for a drink the maid asked for our order, he asked in a rather gutteral voice for a bottle of München, quickly changing it to Whitbreads. With a highly suspicious look the girl disappeared behind the screen, whereupon Greville proceeded to prattle away in semi-subdued German, while I responded with an occasional 'Ja – ja', this being the only German I knew. When we left the old girl must have been hopping mad to think that the fool of an Army officer had let a couple of spies slip through his fingers.

My spy-catching took place when going on leave from my ship on the Clyde to my home in Kent. Whilst having dinner at the Central Hotel, Glasgow (in uniform), I noticed a well dressed young lady at an adjacent table behaving very petulantly with the waiter. Suddenly she leant towards me and said, 'I wonder if you would help me on with my coat. I'm drunk.' As I did so, she told me which train she was catching, and enquired as to my ship. I told her not to ask such questions in wartime, but I was foolish enough to say, in answer to her enquiry, that I was travelling by the same train as she was. She left the restaurant, collected her baggage from the cloakroom, and a porter wheeled it to the platform. A couple of minutes later I went for my bags and was informed by the cloakroom attendant that 'The lady has taken them.'

Hastening in pursuit, I saw her ladyship half-way down the platform with the trolley. I told my porter to go and rescue my bags, which he did, and I dumped them in my reserved sleeping compartment. Standing in the corridor as the train started, I was greeted by a cheery voice saying, 'Ah, here you are!', and taking me by the arm she conducted me to her own sleeper. I was then regaled with descriptions of her family, together with photographs, interspersed with an occasional question regarding myself which I parried suitably, she meanwhile sitting on her bunk and inviting me to sit beside her. This I politely declined, leaning against the doorpost more outside than in, with the door open. I thought I detected the faintest trace of a foreign accent.

Thinking it over behind my own locked door, I concluded that either she was an enemy agent, or else wanting 'a good time' with a reasonable-looking naval officer – or perhaps both. If the former, she might well be responsible at some time or other for the loss of thousands of lives, so I discarded the latter alternative. She had mentioned her name and her husband's occupation, so I called at his professional club to check up. I described her, and asked if the description tallied with Mrs X's appearance. Reluctantly, and after some pressure, I was told, 'That could well be Mrs X.' I then went to Scotland Yard, and reported her and the personal details she had given me. A fortnight later on my way through London, I again called on the Yard and was told, 'Inspector Y is away but asked us to say that he is extremely grateful for your information, and the matter is now in the hands of the military.'

Whilst at Scapa Flow I was put in temporary command for a

weekend or so of a destroyer whose Captain was down south on a Court of Enquiry. Together with *Cossack* (Captain Vian) and one other destroyer, we escorted the battleship *Rodney* for gunnery practice in the Pentland Firth. On completion of this, destroyers were told to return to harbour, and back we sped with *Cossack* in the lead, I next astern. Knowing Captain Vian's rather fierce reputation, I took care to keep accurate station, though he was very parsimonious with signals indicating his speed. We passed through the boom and up Gutter sound at much more than the permitted speed, rocking the boats at other ships' booms as we passed.

We then had to refuel alongside an oiler, *Cossack* on one side, I on the other. I made a good 'alongside', secured my wires quickly and then, perhaps rather tactlessly, crossed over the tanker and watched *Cossack*, with only her bow wire out, trying to manoeuvre her stern in. This took several minutes (to my inward relish!) and when she was secured I asked her First Lieutenant to present my compliments to his Captain and enquire whether he wished me to call on him – a customary courtesy. The curt reply came back: 'No!', delivered by the First Lieutenant with a grin.

On leaving *Punjabi* I was appointed in command of a ship building in Samuel White's yard at Cowes: HMS *Southdown*. I found accommodation at Barton Manor Farm, close to the Osborne estate. An Engineer Officer and a First Lieutenant, to liaise with the firm, had already joined, so there was little for me to do apart from walking down to the ship every day at about noon, have lunch with the firm an hour later, then go back to the farm. The rest of the day was spent farming, which was the best way to recuperate after a gruelling year at sea. Up at six o'clock, a ride round the Osborne estate on the old grey mare before breakfast, then helping Mr George Ablett in a variety of interesting activities: threshing the wheat, learning to thatch ricks, driving the horse plough at one end of the field, while the ploughman drove the tractor at the other end and got me out of difficulty if I needed it. Mrs Ablett insured that I was comfortable and well fed.

The Battle of Britain was in progress at this time and one could see the air raids over Southampton and Portsmouth, the enemy planes often flying low over the farm when making their get-away. One day I went over to Portsmouth and spent the night at a B&B lodging. In the middle of the night there was an air raid alarm and invasion scare. I turned out and went along to the RN Barracks to see if I could be of any use. I found the parade ground packed with men in complete darkness and an impressive silence except for one or two voices giving orders. I was put in charge of the defence of the Guildhall, which included the Lord Mayor and Lady Mayoress. As far as I remember I had a couple of Lewis guns to stick out of an upper window, so I was glad when the invasion part of it proved groundless, and I returned to bed through a hail of falling flak.

At about this time I went to a performance of *King Lear* at the Old Vic, with a superb cast including John Gielgud, Jack Hawkins, Rachel Compton, Kathleen Nesbitt, and Jessica Tandy looking divine in the part of Cordelia. I fell head over heels in love, and decided to take quick action. My plan was to go to a matinée and send my card round backstage inviting her to come for a drink or a cup of tea after the show, knowing that if things went well it could be followed up, but if it was sticky it would not last long, as there would be an evening performance to follow. I went along to Keith Prowse in Bond Street to look up Jessica Tandy in *Who's Who in the Theatre*, so as to be well primed with her history. That publication informed me that she was thirty-one years of age (OK – I was 32) and in 1938 (oh NO!) married Jack Hawkins, who was in the cast!

Before the *Southdown* was completed, I was unexpectedly appointed in command of my old destroyer *Anthony*, seagoing and based at the time on the Clyde. I immensely enjoyed the next few months on convoy work. We escorted the newly built liner *Queen Elizabeth* on her maiden voyage from the Clyde, round the North of Ireland, where we bade her God speed on her way to America. My time in the *Anthony* was all too short, however, as we incurred damage alongside another ship in bad weather which involved docking for some time, and I was appointed to HMS *Repulse* in the Home Fleet at Scapa Flow.

Repulse's Captain (N.R.D. Tennant, later Admiral) was a keen bird watcher and I was told on joining, that he was almost more interested if a bird was sighted at sea than he was in a submarine's periscope! One of my fellow officers was nicknamed The Gawk. He had been on watch at sea one day when a large bird settled on the front of the compass platform. He at once reported it to the Captain, who said, 'Well, what is it?'

Completely at a loss, he replied hesitantly, 'I think it's a lesser gawk, Sir.'

The captain came bounding up the ladder two steps at a time, took one look and in a frigid tone said. 'It's a brown owl.' The Gawk never lived it down.

The new and powerful German battleship *Bismarck* put to sea that summer. The Home Fleet went in search of her. We were in company with the Commander-in-Chief in *King George V* and the aircraft carrier *Victorious*, when we heard that the mighty *Hood* had been sunk engaging the *Bismarck*. The following night the C-in-C signalled that he expected to meet the *Bismarck* at 2am, a formidable prospect for a ship built, as the *Repulse* was, in 1917, and considerably less well armed and protected than the *Hood*. My own nerves, whilst I was cooped up in 'A' turret and feeling rather like a rat in a trap, were stilled by the conviction that the *Bismarck* would avoid us by cutting under our stern and making for Brest, which thankfully was what she did, and was later caught and sunk before getting there.

Repulse had to part company with the C-in-C before the 'kill', due to shortage of fuel, and made for Halifax, Nova Scotia. Captain Tennant only went ashore during the War for one of four things – golf, shooting, fishing or bird watching – and liked an officer to keep him company. As I was the only one on board beside himself with a fishing rod, he arranged for himself and me to have a couple of days fishing whilst in Canada.

We were driven in a luxurious car down to Liverpool, a small village on the river Mersey (!) and accommodated in a log cabin. Each morning a local man came along and drove us up river to a couple of punts, and we fished all day in delightful, peaceful surroundings, being fetched in the evening and given a meal in a small restaurant in Liverpool. Captain Tennant was an expert fisherman but neither of us caught a thing. On being driven back to the ship and unloading the car, we found a long, thin package with our own bags, inside which was a salmon. A nice gesture.

Later in the year the Japanese menace loomed up and the *Repulse* was ordered out to the Far East.

Chapter 6

Ever since Japan's attack on China it had been evident that she coveted the hegemony of the Far East, and the intention was to dissuade her from siding with our enemies by reinforcing the British naval presence.

Our first port of call was at Sierra Leone. Sitting on the verandah of the local hotel, I was intrigued by an Arab fortune teller who had a sheaf of letters from previous clients, including one written on crested ship's notepaper by a friend of mine whose signature I knew well. He had written, 'If Abdul bin Something-or-other has told me my future as accurately as he has told me my past, he is a remarkable fellow.' I declined, happily, to have my future told.

Circumnavigation of Africa included a call at Cape Town, where Jan Smuts came on board and gave a fiery speech to the ship's company. We then called at Mombasa to refuel – and incidentally to enjoy a moonlight bathing party with the local young ladies, organised by our Captain. From there we crossed over to the Seychelles and Trincomalee.

On passage to Singapore I experienced a curious phenomenon. At sunrise one morning when I was on watch, the sun made its appearance on the horizon ahead of us and spread its rays out fanwise, the total appearance being a perfect replica of the flag of Japan. It could well have been taken as an omen of things to come. We arrived at Singapore a few days before the Japanese declaration of war.

Singapore is a natural island lying off the south coast of Johore, but it was joined to the mainland by a causeway constructed before the War. The country to the north is largely thick jungle, and the only attack visualised by the military was by sea. Singapore's sole defences were big guns covering the sea approaches, which in the result were never used.

When the Jap invasion force set out for northern Malaya, the British Admiral, Tom Phillips, had an unenviable decision to make. His sole resource was two capital ships – the old *Repulse* and the newly constructed and recently commissioned *Prince of Wales*, which had scarcely had time to work up properly – and two destroyers, whilst the aircraft carrier which should have joined him had been delayed at Panama.

The coast of Malaya was within striking distance of a Japanese air base, and he was told that if he took his force up the coast, the RAF could only cover him within a limited range of Singapore. The Admiral could hardly have done otherwise than sail to engage the Japs, accepting the air risk. In the event the unbalanced force was attacked by Jap aircraft before we were out of range of our own 'planes. Admiral Phillips, a better Staff Officer than seaman, was known to maintain that a capital ship could well defend itself with its anti-aircraft guns, and in this belief he omitted to report the attack to Singapore. Captain Tennant therefore took it upon himself to report it, and fighter aircraft were sent out, but they arrived too late to be of assistance and both capital ships were sunk.

My action station was 'A' turret (15-inch), but as the main armament would clearly not be required I stayed on the bridge during the attack, first by high bombers which scored one hit, then by torpedo bombers whose first assault was avoided by skilful handling on the part of the Captain, but whose second attack scored three fatal hits. The ship turned over on her side before sinking, which was lucky for those of us on the bridge, who would otherwise have been sucked down the funnel. I went down in a lot of froth and bubbles, surfaced and submerged a couple more times, and finally swam to a Carley raft on which, amongst others, was the Captain. We were picked up by one of our destroyers and spent a long time in the neighbourhood retrieving survivors before returning to Singapore.

With the false sense of security generated by a big battlecruiser, I had kept a good many treasured possessions on board, all of which now lie in Davy Jones's locker at the bottom of the China Sea.

A curious incident remains unexplained. My mother was living at the time in a country inn in North Devon. On the morning of 10th December, the day when *Repulse* was sunk, she woke up to hear the maid coming along the landing with her breakfast tray at 8 o'clock, and at the same time she heard my voice saying, 'It's all right, mother, I'm quite safe,' which, of course, meant nothing to her. When the maid entered the room my mother said, 'Did you hear that voice, Mary?'

'What voice, Mrs Clark?'

'My son's voice.'

'Your son's voice? Of course I didn't, he's thousands of miles away! You must have been dreaming.'

'No, I wasn't. I heard you coming along the landing, and he said quite clearly, "It's all right, mother, I'm quite safe."'

The following afternoon when my mother turned on the wireless for the one o'clock news, she heard Churchill announce the loss of the *Repulse* and the *Prince of Wales*, which was a terrible shock. The maid, Mary, was able to calm her down by reminding her of her experience the previous day. It is of interest that 8am in England is 4pm in Singapore, which would have been about the first time I would have been able to think of anything other than my own surroundings and activity in rescuing survivors.

At about this time a friend who had been in *Repulse* with me gave me a copy of *The Pilgrim's Progress*. I had no time to read it, but my glance did fall on the passage where Faithful says to Christian, 'When thou passest through the waters I will be with thee, and through the rivers they shall not overflow thee.' Nothing could have been more appropriate to the occasion, or more prophetic, as my activities during the next two or three months were confined to 'the waters', which again did all but overflow me, and that text was in my mind later as I swam for a day and a half in danger of my life from sharks, but with complete peace of mind.

After being wrung out and dried ashore I was given the job of Naval Air Liaison Officer at Combined Headquarters in Singapore. Whilst I was there, an Army Officer, Major Angus Rose of the Argylls, and I were gloomily studying the map showing the Japanese invaders and our own retiring forces, reflecting that nothing in the way of offensive action was being taken – all were in retreat. We reckoned that commandos operating up the coast behind the Jap lines could be effective, and together we decided to tackle our respective senior officers, Admiral Spooner and General Percival. The outcome was approval to go ahead. Angus Rose was given a couple of platoons and I was given carte blanche with top priority to pick what craft I wanted, with whatever officers I chose, and to take them up the coast, keeping in direct touch with the Admiral, who promised his full support.

I commandeered a ship, a couple of motor launches and other small craft, and all the officers I wanted except one, whom the Chief of Staff refused to let me have. I pointed out that the Admiral had said I was to have top priority, but the COS irritably replied, 'Oh, the Admiral says that to everyone.' I went to the Admiral and reported that I was all ready except for one officer whom I had not been able to get.

'Why not?' said the Admiral.

'Captain B won't let me have him.'

'Did you tell Captain B that I'd said you were to be given top priority?'

I thought to myself, 'Here goes!' and said, 'Yes, Sir. Captain B said that you say that to everyone.'

The Admiral shot up from his chair, grabbed his cap saying, 'Come with me', and together we tore round in his car to Captain B's office. There, in the presence of his entire staff, Captain B was torn to ribbons by the Admiral and ordered to give me the officer I wanted at once. The Admiral then turned and stormed out of the office, and I took care to hang on to his coat tails!

It was a young officer's dream! In less than a week from getting the go-ahead I was based at Port Swettenham in SS *Kudat* with my small craft. We put in our first raid behind the Jap lines on Boxing Day, blowing up a convoy with a staff car believed to be carrying a Jap general. I was in direct personal contact with the senior Military conducting the retreat, in particular General Heath, General Key and Brigadier Muir, as well as General Percival. But the Japanese advance and the British retreat continued, the *Kudat* was bombed

43

and sunk, and as the Japs lobbed us with their mortars we moved progressively south to Muar and Batu Bahat. Sadly, after a short time the Army removed our troops to stop gaps in their lines, so I had to be content with patrols.

But in the later stages of the retreat, when the Army was retiring on to Singapore Island and troops were again available to me, I was able to organise another raid up the coast. I was on my way, when a wireless telegraph message ordered me to abandon the raid and take all available craft to Sungei Punggor and endeavour to evacuate two thousand British and Australian troops cut off behind the Japanese lines. Sungei Punggor was a stream winding its way across the muddy foreshore, almost dry at low tide, and indiscernible at high water. On arrival we staked out the channel at low water. I had a conglomeration of small craft with me, some having to lie a considerable distance offshore, including the ex-China gunboat *Dragonfly* which was sent to join me and two MLs of 100ft and 72ft. Other small craft were able to move well inshore and at high water could pass up the winding stream. I had one or two shallow-draft native tongkangs too.

The troops were located and evacuation was started – by night only; all craft were sent away at dawn, when the troops lay low in the mangroves, the boats returning at dusk. It was a dangerous situation. We could hear the Jap motor transport racing along the main road, no more than a hundred yards away througn the 'ulu'. An occasional Jap aeroplane passed overhead. One could not help admiring their fighting spirit: their advance down the peninsular was relentless and fast. From the hut from which I controlled the secret operation, I saw Japanes outriders on motor cycles tearing past into territory not yet abandoned by British troops, apparently regardless of personal safety. Their tactics were quietly to penetrate or out-flank our lines – easily accomplished in jungle country – and attack from our rear, attack from both in front and behind being extremely demoralising.

As for our own troops, strict discipline and absolute silence were imposed, all our lives depending on not being discovered. When the tide was high enough, the small craft came up the tortuous stream, the larger, less manoeuvrable ones having to be pushed round the bends by myself and others, wading up to our necks in water. All the troops were evacuated in four nights, and we returned to Singapore. I remember having breakfast on board HMS *Sultan*, tired out, but breakfast has never tasted so good.

On return to the Island I was allotted to Australian Advanced Headquarters as Naval Liaison Officer. I was standing on the lawn outside, when some Jap bombers came over and I saw a stick of bombs coming straight for us. I threw myself flat on the ground. One bomb, with a terrific blast, blew my hat off, ripped the side of my shirt and deafened my right ear, fracturing the ear drum. When the cloud of earth and dust had settled, I stretched out my right hand beyond my head – it was in the bomb hole!

My attachment to Australian Advanced Headquarters enabled me to see a demoralised army in retreat, which I hope I shall never see again. Orders were given by the authorities for priority to be given to women and children, for passage in ships evacuating Singapore. A number of Australian troops endeavouring to force their way on board had to be kept off at the point of the bayonet. An outstanding exception was an Australian brigade commanded by a Brigadier known as Black Jack, whose discipline and behaviour was faultless.

Two days before the surrender, when Singapore was in flames under a canopy of black smoke and everywhere was chaos, Admiral Spooner instructed me to take passage in a motor launch to Java and start up commando raids there when the Japs invaded it. I left in a boat commanded by a young RNVR officer, taking sixty key Army personnel with us. We motored by night, hiding by day, camouflaged against aircraft spotting.

Three days out from Singpore, at dawn actions stations in the Banka Straits, we sighted a warship dead ahead and stern towards us, which we assumed to be a Dutchman. We continued to close her. The signalman reported the 'poached egg' (as we termed the Japanese ensign) flying from her stern, and this unpleasant surprise was confirmed when she turned to port and showed the spoon-shaped bow characteristic of Japanese ships. It was a Japanese destroyer, now a bare half mile away. It was like a mouse running into a cat. At once it was evident that there was no hope of escape; she was capable of travelling at thirty-six knots, and we could just manage eighteen. The young RNVR officer asked me to take over and he himself went and took the wheel. There seemed only one thing to do: close, and give her a dose of pepper before we were sent to the bottom.

The Army personnel on board were told to load their rifles and, together with our little 12-pounder and Lewis guns, all aim at the enemy's bridge, where it was probable that most of their officers gathered. I ordered full speed and, as we passed on opposite courses, both vessels let fly at a distance of about 400 yards. One salvo from her 4.7-inch guns virtually knocked us out; we sustained four, or possibly five direct hits. The fo'c'sle gun was knocked off its mounting, a fire started in the engine room and another below deck forward; the petrol tanks were blazing. The upper deck where about fifty-five key Army personnel had been standing was a bloody shambles, deck and scuppers running with blood, and a horrible sight. My left arm was shattered at the wrist. I altered course in order to position the ship roughly parallel to the enemy, and also to close the Sumatra shore, so that in the almost certain event of being sunk the troops would have an easier swim to the mainland. The wheel jammed hard to starboard and we started turning in a circle at a range of about 1,000 yards, losing speed and clearly starting to sink. Further action, offensive or defensive, was impossible. I stopped engines and ordered 'Abandon ship'.

Casualties were heavy. We quickly did what we could for those who had any chance of surviving, lashing the helpless to planks, and within ten minutes of opening fire the ship sank, burning furiously, with her White Ensign still flying. We had therefore not indicated surrender, but the Japanese destroyer lying off had ceased fire, though it made no attempt to pick up survivors. I advised the men to make for the mainland shore, which was all mangrove swamp. A group of about twelve, nearly all Army, including a Colonel, swam into an abandoned Dutch lifeboat, and clambered aboard.

46

They were fortunate in having with them young Acting Petty Officer Heywood, who had been one of my best sailing coxswains at Shotley and, having survived the sinking of the *Prince of Wales*, had attached himself to me during my commando operations, calling himself my Coxswain. Young Heywood found that the boat was equipped with mast and sails, charts and provisions, so taking charge of the whole party, including the Colonel, he rigged it for sailing and for thirteen days and nights sailed it through the Banka Straits and towards Batavia. Before they could get there they ran into a Japanese manned junk and were taken prisoner. Rotten luck!

Chapter 7

I soon found myself alone in the water with a shattered wrist, and managed to support myself with an empty wooden ammunition box tucked under the useless arm. In the distance I spotted a lighthouse, so I started to swim slowly towards it. The water was warm and I paddled along for about twelve hours, finding myself at dusk close to a native fishing 'pagar' – a bamboo and thatch hut on stilts in shallow water. I climbed up and spent the night in it. At daylight I got into the water again and went on swimming towards the still distant lighthouse, and at about midday came to another fishing pagar, not far from the mangrove swamps, with a man in it who turned out to be an Army officer from the Ordnance Corps – Major Charles Lyddon with even less clothing than I. We joined forces and swam to the mangroves.

I was later told by a Dutch marine biologist that these were the most shark-infested waters in the world. I can only suppose that the recent bombing had driven them away. In any case, my mind was untroubled whilst I was in the water, and greatly sustained by remembrance of the lines from *The Pilgrim's Progress* mentioned earlier.

For six hours we tramped through the mangroves, a muddy business and an agonising one, since mangroves with their sharp roots like inverted carrots are very hard on the feet. We reached a river at dusk and about half a mile downstream we saw a village, so we got into the water again and swam down to it. After a slightly hostile reception we took up our quarters in an empty house (all the houses were on stilts), and were very shortly joined by a Major Bird and a Yorkshire private named Ralph Simpson. Neither here nor at any other time did we get any help from Malays. In our sopping-wet and scanty clothing we were clearly from a defeated force – a fact doubtless confirmed by 'bush telegraph' – and the

Malayan philosphy was to be on the winning side. Moored up in the water beneath us were a number of canoes, so after dark, when all was quiet, we climbed silently down and slipped away in one of them, paddling up river.

The next six or eight days were pretty much like hell, the river being bordered by thick jungle vegetation which effectively prevented any breeze giving us respite from the scorching sun. From time to time, however, some relief was provided by rain, which came down in buckets, soaking us to the skin. My arm meantime had swollen until it looked like a bolster, and the elbow joint had completely disappeared. Major Bird was in a bad way with a strained back and most of the time was in a state of coma. The other two seemed to be in pretty good shape.

had resigned myself to a future as a one-armed Nelson if I survived, but Ralph Simpson was more optimistic and said, 'When I had anything septic, Sir, my granny always put on a soap and sugar poultice', which advice, given in the middle of the jungle, rather amused me. But when in due course we arrived at a clearing with a few native houses, Ralph nipped ashore and in a few minutes came back with a piece of yellow soap, some sugar and some hot porridge rice. Kneading sugar and flakes of soap into a paste he put it on the wound on my wrist, covered it with the hot rice wrapped up in my grubby handkerchief, and bound the whole lot up with one of my stockings.

On landing we were shown an empty house and told we could use it. After discussing the situation we decided that Ralph Simpson and Major Lyddon, both fit men, should proceed up river, whilst Bird (nicknamed 'Oiseau') and I remained to try and recover. Incredibly, after thirty-six hours my arm was down to normal and after forty-eight hours the shrapnel was being sucked out of the wrist. I strapped a piece of board on the forearm and hand, and about two weeks later the broken bone had been repaired and the flesh was re-forming.

We remained in the native hut, keeping ourselves going by eating rubber nuts which lay in profusion underneath, and a mere handful of green beans which the natives gave us. We later discovered that rubber nuts contain a mild poison! After four weeks the natives told us that the Australians had driven the Japs out of Palembang, where there was a hospital and where we could buy some clothes, and they offered to take us in canoes upstream. We accepted this offer, our hope being eventually to get to Bencoolan on the west coast and somehow or other to sea. My intention was to make for India.

We were taken to a point where they said we would have to make our own way through the rimba (deep jungle). An interesting night trek followed: we had to travel over a 'path' made by the trunks of felled trees, with the strange cries of wild animals in our ears. Luckily it was a moonlit night. At the far end we were met by a group of Malays who took us to Palembang. After crossing the river we were put into a small bus and driven to the outskirts of the town. To our surprise and alarm, we stopped at a barrier, at either end of which was a Japanese sentry. We had been led into a trap and were now prisoners – sold for forty guilders a head.

My fellow Prisoners Of War included some that I knew, and a number of these were from the *Repulse* and *Prince of Wales*. In addition there was a small group of Australians and New Zealanders, several officers of the Malayan RNVR and a fairly large number of Dutch, who were always kept separate. For a time we were accommodated in a school building and some adjacent bungalows. Later we were moved to a specially constructed camp in the jungle, made of wood, bamboo and thatch. We slept on beds of bamboo strips.

Our men were required to work on the construction of an aerodrome for the main part, others working at the docks, with our own officers in charge and Japanese guards for company. As senior officer of the main Naval and Royal Marine party I was regarded as their CO. For my excellent First Lieutenant, I had Wallace Kemp, a Malayan RNVR officer. The camp was commanded in the first case by an Indian Army colonel of peppery disposition who was constantly at odds with the Japs, and later by Commander Philip Reid, who had the knack of dealing with our captors in a firm but reasonably co-operative fashion which was essential for our general welfare, if not survival.

I also had charge for some months, before they were moved elsewhere, of about a dozen Malayan RNVR ratings, and made the most of their presence by learning the Malayan language, helped also by some of the British who had been living in Malaya as planters or civil servants before the War. To have some form of physical employment was essential and I occupied my time in gardening for our benefit, taking advantage of the fact that I had a wounded wrist and was unfit for heavier tasks. Those on working parties were frequently able to acquire things from the abandoned Dutch houses, including a supply of good English literature, which was a boon as far as I was concerned. One POW, one of several who became lifelong friends, had a Schofield Reference Bible which was a source of inexhaustible study and which I borrowed frequently. A drawing class was held by a scenic artist who had worked in the theatre world at home.

To call our rations, mainly rice, anything but a slow starvation diet would be a travesty of the truth, and witness to this was not only my weight, which dropped from a normal 12st 10oz to 8st 6oz in the course of imprisonment, but also the fact that during the last six months or so men were dying like flies of beri-beri, malaria, dysentery and sheer malnutrition. Among the victims, sadly, was my old Shotley trainee, Heywood. My own freedom from these killers I can only attribute to a sound constitution.

Red Cross parcels were not passed on to us and letters from home were rare and very restricted in length. My own mother only conveyed to me the news of my decoration for Malayan operations by addressing the envelope to Lt Cmdr V.C.F. Clark, DSC *and Bar*, heavily underlining the 'and Bar'. Our annual postcard home was limited to twenty-five words. One POW is said to have got away with more than that by a eulogy of life under the Japs (splendid accommodation, ample delicious food, kind guards, etc.) adding, 'And you can tell that to the Marines!'

We held a service every Sunday, voluntarily attended by a good number. At the end, instead of singing the National Anthem, which was forbidden, we always sang 'Land of Hope and Glory' with tremendous gusto.

51

The Japs supplied us with a version of news of the War, which invariably consisted of Jap victories and smashing Allied defeats. However, one of the Australians acquired sufficient material when out on working parties to make a wireless set, which he hid and operated inside his mosquito net and on which he was able to get accurate news, mainly, I think, from New Delhi and Australia, so that we did know what was actually happening, which was a great morale booster. But it was unbearably frustrating to be cooped up as a POW, knowing for a time that the War was going against us and later that the tide had turned and victories were being won, and in both cases being unable to take any part, though specifically trained to do so. When the tide did turn and we were ordered for the first time to lie on our bamboo beds for an air raid, some of us were cock-a-hoop to read on the fuselage of a plane flying low over the camp, 'ROYAL NAVY'. Our RAF friends were not so amused!

Apart from the diet we were not badly treated, and I personally was chastised only once – in the early days – perhaps deservedly and certainly understandably. I was leaning on the balcony of our accommodation bungalow on a lovely cool moonlight night, when a Jap sentry came along and barked at me, indicating, as I well knew, that I was to go to bed. I took no notice. After another bark, also disregarded, he came up to me shaking his rifle and fixed bayonet, and indicated that I was to follow him. Between the quarters of the officers and those of other ranks, stood a Sikh sentry. On reaching this point the Jap told me to stay there, standing at attention. The intention was clearly to make a British officer look small in the eyes of the erstwhile British Sikh. I indicated my objections but the Jap just walked away; so I turned back as noisily as I could towards my quarters. The Jap turned round and barked at me. I took no notice. On hearing him running back, shaking his rifle and bayonet, I stopped and signalled that I would not stand where he had put me – either I would return to my quarters or go to the Jap Guard House.

He took me to the Guard House, where for about an hour I was made to stand at attention in the middle of the room where three other Sikhs were sitting. Then the Jap officer in charge came along. Standing in front of me, so close that his chest just about touched my stomach, he looked up at me, barking away in an angry harangue. This he alternated with marching up and down in front of me, imitating the idea he had of the proud British officer, saying as he did so, 'Breetish shoko – Breetish shoko'. Finally he gave me what they humorously termed a 'presento' – a right hook to the jaw! – followed by more barking and a left hook. I managed to retain my feet and after about four blows was told to go. Mustering all the dignity I could I stalked away, giving the Sikhs a stealthy wink, and back to my quarters and to bed.

It is well understood in the Services that if one is captured it is one's duty to escape if humanly possible. No escape was ever made from Palembang, which is surrounded almost entirely by marsh. Escapes made on the Malayan mainland were successful largely due to the widespread Chinese population who, remembering the hostilities between China and Japan a few years before, had no love for the Japanese and were only too ready to assist escapees. One of my fellow POWs was an RAF pilot. I tried to persuade him to make an escape with me from our camp, head for the nearby aerodrome by night, seize one of the 'planes and take off for allied territory. But he appeared to lack the nerve, and declined to make the attempt.

About three months before the end of the War we were transferred to Singapore, packed on the upper deck of a small and ancient steamer, so close that there was no room to lie down. One stood or sat huddled up. The food on passage consisted of bananas boiled without being peeled – or, apparently, washed – the resulting thick black liquid served out being foul enough to turn the strongest of stomachs.

Quarters in the coolie lines at Singapore, in Changi gaol, were luxurious compared with the Palembang camp, and so, by comparison, was the food. The acquisition and promulgation of news was even better than in Palembang. In the gaol was a room given to the making and repairing of medical and surgical instruments by POWs, which contained an old billiard table. A young Army officer had removed one leg, scooped a hole in the top sufficiently big to contain a miniature wireless set which he had made, and then replaced it. On the inner side of the leg was a hole in which he plugged a stethoscope to listen-in. Should a sentry suddenly appear, all he had to do was to pull out the stethoscope and it would appear as one of the many medical and surgical instruments lying on the table. The news was spread quietly in about four stages of geometrical progression before reaching the last of us. The Japs realised that we knew, but they never discovered how.

One day the sentries announced that we were free! It was a tremendous moment, though not entirely unexpected. We all knew how things were going, but our doubt was whether, in the event of an allied landing, the Japs would herd us into the gaol's main enclosure and slaughter us all. Presumably they considered *their* likely fate if they did. The relief was considerable when, with HMS *Sussex* now in the harbour, our guards appeared to adopt a quietly fatalistic attitude, taking no further interest in us.

The Navy were the first to turn up! Then I believe Lady Mountbatten arrived with the Red Cross. We were given complete liberty to leave Changi and to go into Singapore, and the freedom was just glorious. I went into hospital for a week (and how angelic the nurses seemed!) and then decided to go to the temporary hospital at Jalahali near Madras to put on weight in a disciplined way before returning to England. A few silly asses literally gorged themselves to death before they got home, unable to resist the demands of the flesh.

A couple of charming Wren officers were sent up to Jalahali, officially 'to take records' but in fact, I am sure, to provide pleasant company for the few of us who were there, with a bit of social life in Madras. From them I learned that POWs were being sent to England in passenger liners from Bombay. The very idea horrified me and when they told me that a destroyer flotilla would shortly be passing through Colombo on its way home, one of whose Captains and his First Lieutenant I knew, I got them to arrange for me to fly to Colombo and await its arrival.

The only snag was that the limit of one's baggage by air was ninety pounds, and hearing of the shortages in England I had been

54

busily buying up Madras, until my stuff weighed something like twenty stone. My splendid Wrens, however, were undismayed, merely saying, 'Leave it to us', and when I arrived at the aerodrome and my mountain of belongings was wheeled on to the weighing machine, the RAF officer did a quick calculation and wrote down on his form, 'Weight of officer's baggage 90lbs. Officer's personal weight 20 stone' – and there I stood as thin as a scarecrow!

At Colombo another Wren officer took me dinghy sailing for a couple of days whilst awaiting the arrival of the destroyers. Commander de Chair of the *Venus* and his First Lieutenant, Peter Maryon, gladly accepted me as a working passenger to England, providing me with uniform, and allowing me to keep watch. By the time we reached Devonport, I had really been put back on my feet.

Chapter 8

Their Lordships wisely gave such as myself a good bit of leave in which to recuperate after our three and a half years as POWs. This I spent at home with my mother, living at Burton Latimer within a couple of miles of my brother Gordon's rectory at Barton Seagrave in Northamptonshire. Katie Bridges, the tenant of one of the Rectory cottages, kept horses in his stables and helped my recuperation greatly by mounting me for hacking and occasional hunting with the Woodland Pytchley.

I was then given command of the frigate *Loch Tralaig* in the Anti-Submarine flotilla at Londonderry. That suited me admirably, as we did more sea time than any other unit in the Navy, and the large complement of Wrens in the barracks was a big contribution to the enjoyment of our free time. Moreover there was no difficulty in crossing the border into Donegal, where rationing was unheard of and a nice juicy steak obtainable for the asking. Good riding, too, could be had, and I made the most of that. I hired from a man named Crotty, who supplied me with a horse shaped more like a dachshund than anything else but which sailed over the banks and ditches so beautifully that I might have been sitting in an armchair.

As the senior Commanding Officer under the Commander (D), later Captain (D) of the flotilla, I was acting as Divisional Commander, so just as I had felt I was on the crest of a wave in Malaya in 1942 shortly before I was taken prisoner, so again I felt on the crest of a wave in this appointment. But once again misfortune struck.

I was on passage from the Clyde to Londonderry and decided to side-step and anchor for a few hours off Skipness to the north of the Isle of Arran, where close connections of mine at Skipness

Castle had a house party. I knew the locality quite well and I instructed my Navigating Officer to approach on a certain transit which would clear the buoy marking the spit of rock off Skipness Point.

As we passed the buoy at the expected distance, close to starboard, my Navigating Officer said we were to the north of the transit line. I at once altered course to port, but had scarcely done so before we came to a grinding halt, and looking over the side we could clearly see the rocks below. The Asdic dome was carried away, and the compartment was holed. Putting the engines to 'Full astern' failed to move her and we were on a falling tide. A submarine exercising nearby endeavoured to haul us clear, but it was no good. I had to report my predicament to Londonderry and Glasgow, and the latter sent tugs which towed us off on the flood tide and took us to dry dock in Glasgow.

The sickening part of it was that the buoy, which had recently been taken away for cleaning by the Clyde Lights Trust, had been replaced 800 feet out of position and my brother-in-law at the Castle knew it but forgot to warn me when I had spoken to him on the 'phone. *Loch Tralaig*'s code name for R/T was 'Little Tern' and despite the seriousness of the situation I could not resist sending a signal to my Commander (D) in Londonderry: 'No wonder. According to my bird book the little tern nests in rocks and other stony places.' I never had any comment, but I don't think he was at all amused, perhaps not surprisingly. At the Court of Enquiry I received a severe reprimand, which was the least I could expect, and the very next day I was appointed in command of the sister ship *Loch Dunvegan* with the same job in the A/S flotilla, so I thought I had got away with it. But I hadn't.

Twelve months later, when I confidently expected promotion, I was passed over, and strong protests by my Captain (D), Captain Gibbs and NOIC Londonderry, Captain Onslow, drew the response from the Second Sea Lord that I was being passed over because I put my ship aground and no more was to be said about it. As far as I know the Admiral at Rosyth, whose responsibility it was to oversee navigational aids in this area, did nothing to accept responsibility or clear me. His own yardarm was, perhaps, of more concern!

I was relieved of command shortly afterwards.

I left my ship in the depths of depression. All my lifelong hopes and ambitions were smashed. I would never rise in the Service higher than I was and I would never again go to sea. Captain 'Dickie' Onslow was an understanding man and realised how I felt. I went to say goodbye to him and as I left his office he called me back, saying:

'Victor, I'm going to do something which I'm not supposed to do. I'm going to show you your confidential report by Captain Gibbs, because I don't think I have ever seen one like it.'

I read it in amazement. For every personal characteristic he had given me '9', which was the highest possible, and at the end of his remarks, which were full of praise, he had written 'I consider this Officer should be promoted immediately' – in red ink. To write that, knowing that the Second Sea Lord had personally 'written me off' was courageous. But the fact was that one could not get away with a grounding just after the War, when the Navy was being run down and every opportunity was taken to reduce numbers. Nevertheless, Captain Onslow's understanding act meant that I left his office with my head high. But I could not help thinking that for the Second Sea Lord, who did not know me from Adam, to jam my further promotion after the strongest possible protests from the two Senior Officers who knew me best, did not reflect well on the promotional system – and certainly not on the Second Sea Lord personally.

I spent the rest of my naval career as Chief Training Officer at Sea Cadet Headquarters in London. Five years like a bird in a cage. My creative energy was dissipated in routine paperwork, smothered by pettifogging detail, sidetracked by countless inter-ruptions throughout each day, harassed by the constant ringing of the telephone and the never-ending din of the traffic outside, and finally frustrated by some committee or other.

Whilst cooped up in London I read *Deep Water and Shoal*, the account of the American Robinson's voyage round the world in a

33-foot ketch. It fired my imagination and rekindled my love of the sea, and I followed it up by reading books by Slocum, Pidgeon, Bernicot and others who had made similar voyages. I made up my mind that when I retired I would do the same, so I carefully noted and recorded under various headings their experience in fitting out and running their boats.

Six or seven months before retiring I started looking for a suitable craft. My first visit was to Captain Sullivan, the yacht broker at Captain O.M. Watts' chandlery in Albemarle Street.

'What can I do for you, Sir?' in a delightful Irish accent.

'I want a boat to sail round the world in.'

Without any hesitation he pulled a sheet of paper out of a pigeon-hole, with a photograph on it.

'That's the boat for you, Sir.'

The name was *Solace*, a 33-foot ketch belonging to Lord Stanley of Alderley. The price was £1,800. I said it was too much. Captain Sullivan showed me several other specifications, but with each one pointed to *Solace*, saying 'But *that's* the boat for you, Sir.'

I wrote to a number of brokers, one of whom, after I had returned to him some twenty specifications, told me I was a most discouraging client. About six months after I had started my search I went down to Cowes and saw *Solace* lying in a mud berth at low water, high and dry with the whole of her hull visible. I went on board. She was a little beauty, with pretty lines and a quaint pillared taffrail, and I fell in love with her. She had been pronounced in sound condition generally. I told Captain Sullivan I would give £1,250 but could not afford any more. The bargaining between Captain Sullivan and Lord Stanley went on for several days and finally Lord Stanley said 'Well, if he won't give any more, let him have it.' So in late July 1953 *Solace* became mine.

My plans were well worked out by now and I quickly put her into Smith and Marshall's yard at Lymington for alterations and a general refit. I prepared for the worst, by strengthening the coach roof and fitting extra storm shutters, weather boards and water-tight hatches. I made the cockpit self-draining and greatly increased the capacity of the freshwater tanks. The internal ballast was secured so that, in the event of capsizing, my meditations as I sat on the skylight would not be disturbed by a shower of pig-iron from the keel above me. The upper deck was fitted with twelve-inch lifelines from stem to stern. All these changes were to prove invaluable.

I was joined by 'Chich' Thornton, a friend from my Navy days, who was far more experienced than I in handling yachts. We were pleased to find, on a trial run to Guernsey, that *Solace* sailed herself perfectly on the wind, without any attention to the helm.

It was essential to sail before the equinoctial gales. As September approached, my mother visited *Solace* for the first time and said:

'You're not going to cross the Atlantic in *that*?'

'Yes, I am. Why not?'

'Well, you must be *mad – absolutely MAD*!'

It was suggested that the ship should be blessed before sailing. This idea appealed to me as a naval officer, as all Her Majesty's ships are blessed when first launched, so I arranged for my brother Gordon to conduct a brief ceremony, which he did most impressively.

At last September 4th, the intended day of departure, arrived. I regret to recall that the mountain of stores on the jetty was not stowed in time, so it was on the following morning at 9am that Chich and I waved farewell to our friends. It was a fine day and by a scarcely hoped-for piece of good fortune a breeze from the south-east favoured us. We wished that we had not arranged to put into Plymouth for letters, as the wind was fair for Ushant, but by 6.45 that evening we were passing the famous Barbican steps under all plain sail, with the Blue Ensign flying at the mizzen and the RNSA burgee at the main, leaving Drake's home behind us and bound for his hunting ground, the Indies.

Author with mother – brother Gordon with father.

Author sitting –
Gordon standing.

Author with father (Lord Mayor's Chaplain) leaving Buckingham Palace after attending the only Levee held by Edward VIII.

Author on motorbike 'Sarah', Malta.

HMS *Watchman* in the Bay of Biscay, January 1934.

On the equator, off West Africa, 1941. Watching altitude sight being taken on HMS *Repulse*.

HMML 311 (photograph by kind permission IWM).

Solace lying on Palmerston reef after the storm.

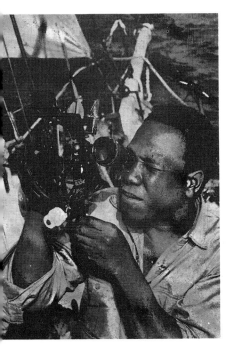

Stanley practises with sextant.

Author in Bantry Bay on return from circumnavigation, August 1959. Brian Craig in background.

Training ship *Prince Louis* under shortened sail.

Training ship *Captain Scott* in Loch Linnhe, Scotland.

Above: *Captain Scott* – hoisting the mainsail.

Right: Danae, giving a helping hand at the Great Yorkshire Show, Harrogate, 1960.

Above: After the wedding. The bridesmaids are Sally and Lucy Saunt, nieces to the bride.

Left to right: Rosalind, Author and Jessica, with their dog Miggs. The girls are in their Christ's Hospital School uniforms.

Chapter 9

For the next few days, fair weather took us west. We were able to try out the self-steering arrangements under twin staysails. It was experimental now, but on many subsequent occasions it became a necessity.

Ten nights or so later I was standing in the forehatch, and watching my little ship cleaving her way up the siver pathway thrown by the light of the moon. Listening to the soughing of the breeze and the thresh of the bow-wave, I felt a great peace. Presently the sun came up and shone with a sub-tropical warmth which drew from our bones the accumulated damp and murk of our northern clime. The fragrance of the air seemed to lead us on with its foretaste of tropical delights to come.

After calling at Madeira, we intended to make direct for Barbados, but we ran into foul weather and a sudden squall snapped one of the mizzen shroud-plates. Inspection showed that it had been made of cast brass, so I reluctantly decided to put into the Canaries and have all the shroud-plates removed and replaced with steel. On the morning of October 20th we left Las Palmas and by the 24th there was every indication from sea and sky that we had at last picked up the trade winds.

It was as well that we were able to set the self-steering, as we were both unwell. I had ear-ache, and Chich became afflicted with a complaint which first kept him frequently on the move and then went into reverse, making it desirable that he should keep more on the move. He attributed both conditions to my diet and cooking. Chich recovered, but after six days of ear-ache I decided to seek medical attention in St Vincent, a most aggravating interruption to our progress but, when facing 2,000 miles of sea to Barbados, the only sensible alternative.

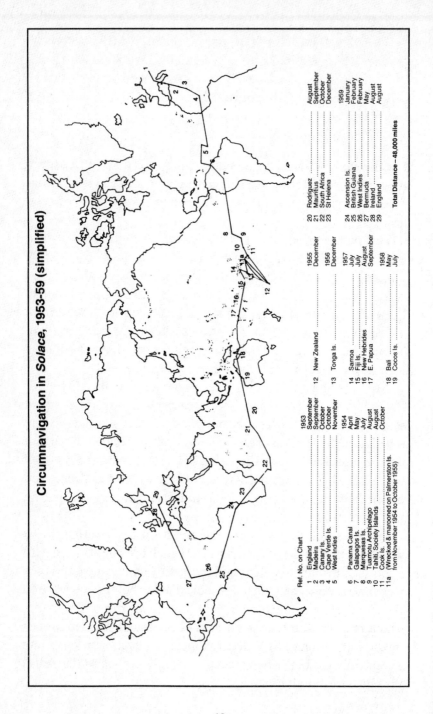

Circumnavigation in *Solace*, 1953-59 (simplified)

Ref. No. on Chart

1	England	1953
2	Madeira	September
3	Canary Is.	September
4	Cape Verde Is.	October
5	West Indies	November
		1954
6	Panama Canal	April
7	Galapagos Is.	May
8	Marquesas Is.	July
9	Tuamotu Archipelago	August
10	Tahiti, Society Islands	August
11	Cook Is.	October
11a	(Wrecked & marooned on Palmerston Is. from November 1954 to October 1955)	

12	New Zealand	1955 December
13	Tonga Is.	1956 December
14	Samoa	1957
15	Fiji Is.	July
16	New Hebrides	July
17	E. Papua	August
		September
18	Bali	1958 May
19	Cocos Is.	July

20	Rodriguez	August
21	Mauritius	September
22	South Africa	October
23	St Helena	December
		1959
24	Ascension Is.	January
25	British Guiana	February
26	West Indies	February
27	Bermuda	May
28	Ireland	August
29	England	August

Total Distance — 48,000 miles

62

We dropped anchor off the port of Mindela, which was desperately poor and disease-ridden. The authorities arrived alongside, with the warning that water-thieves were very active in those parts, and bringing a nightwatchman. His name, I have good reason to remember, was Pedro. I engaged him on the spot, doped myself with aspirin, and opened the hatches to let in the night air.

Woken by a stabbing pain hours later, I was startled by footsteps right over my head. Pedro in the cockpit was huddled in sleep. I peered out through the companion-way to see two dark figures crouching over the fo'c'sle. I thumped Pedro in the midriff. He awoke with a yell, and the intruders went straight over the side into a waiting boat.

Had they taken anything? What?

Chich was awake by now and I told him to check the fo'c'sle to see what was missing, and dashed to get the dinghy; but Pedro had hailed a passing boat with two oarsmen.

I jumped in. 'Row like hell!' I said, and they understood. The race was on. Chich's voice floated over the water: 'Two sails, fifty-fathom coil of rope, oven, pots of paint, bottles of linseed oil, turpentine, varnish . . .'

My crew hurled blood-curdling threats at the flying foe, who replied with solid objects. A stone as big as my fist landed in the bilges.

'Crew say afraid the boat get holes,' said Pedro.

'Twenty escudoes each if they catch 'em!' I bellowed.

The effect was electric: the oars literally bent under the strain. After a mad chase around some coal lighters, we began to close with the enemy, who headed for the rocky shore. Shining my torch on them revealed that they were dropping things overboard. A bottle of my own linseed oil landed in our boat, whilst other missiles hurtled around us.

Both boats grounded simultaneously about ten yards apart. I leapt out in the dark into a pool up to my neck and scrambled out, my sopping pyjamas streamlined to me. Shouts and counter-shouts were deafening. We dashed on over the brow of the hill, and I ordered a 'fan search': 'Go on, full speed, zigzagging for five

63

minutes, shout if you see anyone, come back the same way if you don't.' On we all went, and back we all came! I had a feeling the enemy was pretty near. 'Right! Back to the boats.'

As we retraced our steps Pedro fell over a prone figure. We prodded and pinched it, but there was no reaction. 'Better don't say nothing 'bout him, Captain,' Pedro said nervously, but I decided we had better carry him with us. However the condition of my bare feet was now so bad that I had to put him down at the foot of the cliff, and we made our way to the boats. One of my crew now had charge of both, and I was relieved to find that most of the stolen articles were in the re-captured one. After towing it over to Chich, I went straight inshore, still in my pyjamas. I visited the police, who were apathetic, and the British Consul, who at 4am took some rousing but eventually, after some strong words from me, did all that I requested, and by midday the remaining three villains had been rounded up.

Our stove and, most seriously, our coil of rope were still missing. I visited the Chief of Police, with the suggestion that he question all three men in separate rooms, to find out if they were lying, and to threaten them with punishment if they did not tell the truth. In two hours' time the coil of rope was lying on the floor before me.

The fourth man was indeed dead, and I suspected that he had been poisoned by my turpentine, which I kept in beer bottles, but a post-mortem revealed a more prosaic cause: heart failure. We had chased him to death.

★   ★   ★

After this bare-footed adventure, I needed medical attention at both extremities, and under the care of Dr Fonseca at one end and Dr Alfio at the other I soon felt ready to put to sea. Before we sailed, Dr Fonseca came on board to have a look at *Solace* and arrived carrying a black puppy of four months under his arm. Any doubts I may have had about adding to my crew were quickly dispelled in a smother of excited licks. Yo-yo was clearly pleased with his sailing orders.

But the famous trade wind now let us down badly. My memory of that Atlantic crossing is one of hot days, winds shifting and variable but mainly light, and of constant changing of sails and frustrated, irritable tempers – certainly on my part. The twin stay-sails worked less well in light winds, and we were obliged to steer under all plain sail for much of the time.

I have often been asked by landsmen 'What do you find to do all day?', but when there are only two of you on a boat, there is no time to get bored. When steering by hand, each of the crew is on the tiller for twelve hours a day, and needs eight hours sleep. In the remaining four hours he must cook, serve meals, wash up, clean ship, refit gear and navigate. If he has any time or energy left for reading, writing and general relaxation, he is lucky. At sea plenty of sleep is essential. Steering is tiring, and the constant motion of the ship causes a continual drain of energy even though you may not be aware of it. After three weeks at sea we watched with growing eagerness our position on the chart approaching land. At 6 o'clock on the evening of November 29th we sighted Barbados ahead. It was a great thrill. Whenever I had been asked when I expected to reach the West Indies I had replied, 'By the end of November.' Not a bad estimate!

Members of the Royal Barbados Yacht Club took us under their wing and showed us places of interest. Barbados was our first tropical island and the temptation to linger was strong, but Chich had to be back in England by mid-January, and wished to see more of the West Indies, so I left the programme for the next three weeks to him. We visited St Vincent, the Grenadines, Grenada (where the engine stopped functioning, but I never had much time for engines), and Trinidad. Here we had to make arrangements for Chich's return passage. An Admiralty tanker bound for Gibraltar seemed the best bet, and by great good luck its destination was altered at the last moment to the UK. Chich was duly shipped home.

His place was taken by Brian Greig, who arrived by 'plane from England to join me for a month. Fresh from his moorings in Lincoln's Inn, Brian found the spanking breeze which carried us to Tobago too much for his sea-legs for a while. But as we travelled northwards once more, to reach St Lucia, I thought that the breezy sailing, lovely islands, and quiet secluded anchorages which we found must have chased the stale air of Chancery Lane from every corner of his lungs. Swimming in translucent water, sunbathing on the almost white sand, fishing, exploring the reefs in a dinghy, or going for a romp ashore with Yo-yo – who can tell me of a better rest cure?

After Brian·s departure I moved *Solace* to a small creek which I always called Ganter's Creek, since Mr Bert Ganter had recently erected a boat-repair yard there. From now on I intended to sail single-handed, and accordingly I had some alterations made which needed Bert's assistance. His staff included two men who had set out from England on round-the-world voyages, but had been compelled to abandon their projects. During my voyage I passed a regular string of such once-hopefuls, some of whom had run out of money, some had had crew trouble, some damage to the ship or even wreck, and some had changed their minds on discovering that it is harder work than they had thought.

My own plans were modified despite myself. Commander Milbourne, the Harbour Master, said that a boy he knew and liked was mad keen to go to sea. Would I take him? No, thanks. He begged me to see the lad, who was well educated and had ambitions to skipper his own schooner one day. That interested me. He came to see me, I liked the cut of his jib, I liked his persistence, and after a two-day trial cruise down the coast, Stanley Mathurin, aged sixteen and three-quarters, was taken on as crew. Despite the foibles and eccentricities of his skipper, not to mention his irascibility and impecuniosity, Stanley remained the proud and loyal crew for over five years, becoming the first of his race to circumnavigate the world in a two-man ship.

My resolve to continue into the Pacific, which had not definitely been made on leaving England, had been slowly crystallizing, and I had by now made up my mind to go on. I must aim at passing through the Panama Canal and crossing the Gulf of Panama as soon as possible, before the favourable winds and currents failed.

Heading for English Harbour, Antigua, whence the trip to Jamaica would be due westwards, we coasted up Guadeloupe, a mountainous, sombre island. The weather worsened, and during the night the staysail split and Stanley had the job of handing it and setting the storm staysail during a squall, which he did without any fuss. It was his first real test as a deckhand, and I felt considerable confidence in him afterwards.

English Harbour is, perhaps, the most historic spot in the West Indies. I am not ashamed to say that it was one of the thrills of my life to be taking my own ship *under sail* into the harbour which for three years was Nelson's base, and in and out of which he must have sailed HMS *Boreas* many times. The uncrowned king and queen of English Harbour were Commander and Mrs Vernon Nicholson, who had started a yacht-chartering business in the derelict dockyard, and who were my strength and stay for the next six weeks.

Solace needed a refit badly. I could scarcely believe my eyes when I saw the deterioration which had been wrought by sea, sun and air in the short space of four and a half months in the tropics. Paintwork was chipped and stained, varnish for the most part non-existent, ropes frayed and worn, wire rigging and ironwork rusty – although all of it was new six months before. Sails were in need of repair.

Despite the hard work on board, it was impossible to become completely engrossed when surrounded by fascinating objects and buildings. One of the best preserved buildings is the Admiral's House, used by Captain Horatio Nelson as his residence when he was acting Commander-in-Chief. In the upper rooms are some four-poster beds, in one of which he doubtless slept. In adjacent rooms are a quaint zinc-lined bath in which he must have cooled himself on many a sweltering day, and an ancient commode on which he undoubtedly sat.

Most of the island's village houses were tiny wooden shacks. I went one day with a local lorry-driver to see a house removal. It was all so simple. The family and relations (numbered in dozens) gathered round and lifted the house with spars on to rollers. It was then manoeuvred onto the road, and one end was chocked up sufficiently for the vehicle to back under it. It was levered up and slid onto spars lying across the lorry. The family hopped in, and off we drove. I sat next to the driver, nervously watching the load towering above us. The roof caught in telephone wires and the whole structure wobbled with every bump in the road. I found myself making calculations of critical angles and limiting frictions and wondering at what point I should jump out and save myself. However, we got there, and within a few minutes the house was placed and interchange of social courtesies between the new neighbours had started. By the time we left the mother was cooking a meal as unconcernedly as if they had lived there all their lives.

Five weeks at English Harbour and *Solace* was looking like new. Her captain and crew could feel proud of her once more. It was mid-March, and, with the season getting late, it was time to bid farewell to our kind friends and be off. Mrs Nicholson had seen to it that we were well provisioned, and as the fresh breeze swept us clear of the wharf, she called out anxiously 'Are you all right for money? How much have you got?'

'Fourpence.'

'Horrors! Let me give you some.'

'No. That'll do. No stops between here and Jamaica.'

Chapter 10

The third member of our crew, Yo-yo, deserves a page or two to himself. He had a thick black coat with a white tie, rather stuck-up ears, a straggly tail and, when fully grown, a waterline length of approximately fourteen inches and tonnage about twelve pounds. Not a prizewinner at Crufts, perhaps, but then Yo-yo would have felt as much at home there as would the Ancient Mariner at a tea-party. Chich had referred to him as 'that ugly little mongrel', so I invented a breed and told everyone that he was a Cape Verde Terrier. No-one but a Cape Verde Islander would have been able to argue the point.

He got his name from an attractive little habit of sitting up on his hind legs when he was pleased and waving his front paws up and down – a motion somewhat similar to bouncing a yo-yo. As far as I knew it was a natural expression of delight, and it was certainly a delight to watch. Yo-yo *may* have been no more full of fun and spirits and no more fond of his master than any other little dog, though *I* think he was, and his welcome on my return, if I had to go ashore without him, even if I was away for only twenty minutes, was as if he had not seen me for months. It started the moment he recognised the dinghy approaching and did not subside until every limb within jumping reach had been covered with paws and licks.

Yo-yo was a character – what sort of a character I will leave you to decide. He found his sea-legs immediately. My dealings with the new trainee were based on the motto: 'Begin as you intend to continue'. A small orange-box which fitted tightly between the cockpit coaming and the taffrail pillars, lined with an old pair of trousers, served as his bunk. He was not allowed below, and was perfectly happy on deck, wet or fine. From a hot sun he found shelter in the cockpit; when it rained he was invited below, but usually scorned the invitation. For his daily 'visit to the aunt' he would trot up to the fo'c'sle.

A problem that had to be early overcome was the danger of Yo-yo getting entangled in the sheets and other gear during evolutions such as tacking or anchoring. So he was trained to go to 'Action Stations' – underneath the dinghy which was stowed bottom up on the cabin top. There, with his little nose poking out, he would watch the evolution and emerge on completion. 'Catch-as-catch-can' was his favourite dog-watch exercise, and he seemed to think that that particular watch was named specially for him. As regular as clockwork, if I did not start the game, he would throw out a challenging bark in an attitude of semi-retreat. If I chased him, well and good, but if I felt lazy I had only to make a single motion and he would scamper aft, leap over the cockpit, back over the cabin top, snap at me and tear away on another lap, yelping the while.

Never a fish rose within a quarter of a mile without Yo-yo spotting it and barking. A school of porpoises would send him charging wildly up and down from stem to stern. If a flying-fish landed on deck, Yo-yo would be on it like a flash and stand over it barking in a puzzled, intermittent sort of way which seemed to say, 'I'm not sure what this is doing here, but come and get it before it goes overboard again.'

Before you award Yo-yo the prize for the perfect little sea-dog, I must confess that he was not the paragon of virtue which I may have led you to believe. He was a born thief, and in this disgracefully low enterprise his high IQ was conspicuously evidenced. Not until captain and crew were to all appearances fast asleep, would Yo-yo emerge from his own bunk, creep over the cockpit coaming and jump softly down to the bridge deck. There I remember watching him stand in the companionway, peering in the dark first at my bunk, then at Stanley's, then again at mine, and, satisfied that all was well, slip down onto the engine casing and creep stealthily into the corner where the 'larder' was. How was Yo-yo to know that, outlined against the sky astern, his every movement on the bridge deck could be seen? But he was now in complete darkness, and I got up and switched on the light. There was the oblivious Yo-yo, his nose and eyes immersed in a large tin of butter. I took careful aim and gave his behind the biggest wallop it had ever had. He was out of the cabin like greased lightning.

Of Yo-yo's shoregoing habits the less said the better. Some of the more sordid, such as rolling in dirt, we tried hard to cure. Sometimes Stanley would give him a pep talk before going ashore – on self-discipline, Royal Naval tradition and so on. Yo-yo would sit and look so meek and penitent, as if butter would not melt in his mouth – even tinned butter, but the dinghy scarcely touched shore before Yo-yo was away and streaking down the jetty, deaf to my thunderous cries and heading straight for the nearest rubbish-heap. He was a fine sea dog, but ashore – a hopeless case.

My fortnight's stay in Kingston was an extremely pleasant one. The town itself, like any commercial port, had no natural attraction for me, but I had only the Panama Canal between me and the Pacific, and Kingston afforded almost the last opportunity for stocking up. I had introductions from friends at home, and HMS *Sheffield*, flagship of the North America and West Indies Station, arrived in time for the start of the MCC *v*. West Indies Test Match. To meet one of HM ships always gave me as big a kick as anything on the voyage, for the Navy is my spiritual home. In this case there was the added pleasure of finding some old friends and shipmates on board, who gave me the chance of seeing something of this beautiful island.

By mid-April *Solace* was under way again. As we approached Colon, the accuracy of our course could be confirmed from that of the merchantmen northward bound from the Panama Canal. Limon Bay, which contains the harbour of Colon and Cristobal, is the anchorage at the northern, Atlantic end of the Canal. Fifteen square miles in area, it is entered through a channel between two long breakwaters, which even at night is an almost uninterrupted stream of traffic. I felt like a small boy trying to squeeze through the London Underground barrier in the rush-hour. Half an hour after midnight we sailed in through the breakwaters and anchored comfortably under their lee.

Early next morning I experienced American efficiency. A boat came alongside and discharged its entire contents into the cabin of *Solace* – the doctor, representatives of the Harbour Master, the Police and the Customs, and a fifth whose particular duty I cannot remember and who sat blocking light and air in the companion-way. All of them were enormous, wore horn-rimmed spectacles, carried sheaves of papers and gave crushing handshakes. It was a hot day within a few degrees of the Equator, and after three minutes of a five-fold battery of questions, they were beginning to feel that a small boat without air-conditioning was no place for a respectable citizen of the US. The doctor mopped his streaming brow, his spectacles covered in mist. 'Heck! Sign this and let me get out. I guess you're O.K.!' The others hurriedly followed him.

Solace passed through the Panama Canal on 1st May. A pilot is compulsory, however small the craft. The Canal can be said to be in three sections: the Atlantic level, the Gatun Lake, and the Pacific level. Ships are raised to the Gatun Lake by a series of locks. The best way for a yacht to go through is alongside a banana boat, which is well fendered and accustomed to the procedure. I could not find one, so I lay astern of a large cargo vessel, secured in the middle of the lock by four three-inch lines. The first lock was awe-inspiring. When the floodgates opened, it was as though Niagara had burst in. We were bobbing on the surface of a seething cauldron, straining at the warps. In the second and third locks we were lucky and secured alongside banana boats. The big ships were being towed through with electric mules, but *Solace* moved through under her own motor, which at this juncture was functioning.

The Gatun Lake was originally a jungle swamp. When the Canal was constructed its river exits were dammed and the level raised. As we motored through the well beaconed channel we passed the dead stumps of many semi-submerged jungle trees, and, as they frequently do, my thoughts dwelt on the history of these parts. Were we passing over the spot where Drake captured the Spanish gold train? We were at the very least close to the route by which a constant stream of mules carried gold from Panama across the Isthmus to load into the galleons of the King of Spain.

Some of the moments in my life which stand out most vividly in my memory are those when I have burnt my boats and been thrown on my own resources, either because I have been forced to or because I have voluntarliy chosen to do so. At such times I have always had the feeling of being completely cut off, materially speaking, from what has gone and is now past, and that I (or the group of which I am a part) am on trial for exactly what I am worth. I had such a feeling when, in HMS *Repulse*, we sailed from Singapore well knowing the task and that there were no cover or reserves. I had it when, in command of my little fleet of ships, I had to land behind the enemy lines in Malaya.

It is a great moment when a man meets with a challenge and if he accepts it, coolly and deliberately, finds that acceptance brings all that is necessary to meet it – an unsuspected strength of spirit, courage, alertness, determination, faith and peace of mind. I had felt that on leaving the shores of England. I felt it again now. The Isthmus of Panama seemed like a wall over which I had jumped. My communications with home and civilization were finally cut. Before me lay the vast expanse of the biggest ocean in the world, in all its loneliness, its hidden dangers and its cruelty, and with all its strangeness and beauty.

Chapter 11

The Gulf of Panama and the waters for several hundred miles to seaward of it are surely one of the worst areas in the world for sailing – one day in three a flat calm, the remainder seldom more than a light breeze, at all times squally and frequently raining in bucketsful. Study of the wind chart was very depressing, reports from people with local knowledge equally so. I decided that the best route would be due south from Cape Mala until within sight of the coast of Ecuador, then to make sou'-westing until the south-east trade wind was picked up, which would carry me to the Galapagos Islands, my first port of call.

Twelve days later I made my last attempt on any passage to start the engine, wasting from three to six in the morning on the job and failing to get a murmur. So I resigned myself to faith, hope and as much charity as I could muster with a very frayed temper, whilst Stanley tried his hand at baking bread. It was his first attempt, using a small rectangular biscuit-tin and a Prestige Wonder Oven on a primus, and the result was an unqualified success.

On the 19th May we crossed the Line, having made good only 200 miles in nine days, though we had covered 500 through the water, but the wind was backing and things looked more hopeful. With a two-man crew, there are formidable difficulties in maintaining the time-honoured traditions. Faced with the prospect of having to combine the functions of Neptune, Amphitrite, their Court and the Bears, I'm afraid I gave it up, and we just 'spliced the mainbrace'.

We were now entering the Humboldt Current, and found it cold by both day and night. We wore duffle coats on deck, and encountered fog, strong currents and flat calm, but we made a perfect landfall. The Galapagos are volcanic islands, brown and arid in appearance, but the waters are probably as full of life as any in the world. A school of porpoises crossed our bow, a seal came gambolling round, and several frigate birds, gliding overhead, took a delight in attacking my RNSA burgee – fortunately old and battered. We passed close to Kicker Rock, a 500-foot geological freak like a suet pudding with a slice cut right through the middle of it. The gap is not more than thirty feet wide; I resisted the temptation to motor through it, and we passed by. We anchored in Wreck Bay at Chatham Island.

To my surprise we were boarded by a couple of naval officers, who informed me that this was a base of the Ecuadorean Navy. I had no visa, because I would not pay the exorbitant price demanded at Panama, but despite this we were warmly welcomed and invited to make use of all the facilities that the base could offer. There was a statue of Charles Darwin, his corroding bust resting on a cracking cement pedestal occupied by a distant four-footed relative of his – a lizard!

At Wreck Bay I met Karin Cobos, the Norwegian wife of Manuel Cobos, whose father and ancestors used to own this island. Mounted on the Cobos's horses, I was accompanied by one of her sons to their house, built to Karen's design in Norwegian style on the grassy upper slopes. The ride was a test of endurance as well as a pleasure, since the road resembled a rocky river bed and to carry a rider safely along it a horse has to be locally bred. The soil underfoot was red brown, the road was lined with green bushes and rather fewer trees, the hinterland was grey-green scrub. At some points tall orange trees hung over and littered the ground with golden fruit. Higher up, the countryside took on a fresh look; you could imagine you were riding on Dartmoor. Here we could trot and canter, and the cool air was exhilarating beyond measure. The slopes were dotted with cattle and horses belonging to Karin, whose house we could now see – Campo Mio. She is undoubtedly of the stuff of which heroines are made, and I had to admit to more than a touch of envy for the life she had cut out for herself.

The pleasant stay at Wreck Bay was marred by one very sad

event. One evening after dark Yo-yo had a fit and dashed all over the ship barking madly. Before I could get some pills he had jumped overboard. Swimming and struggling with a semi-mad dog in the dark, in a sea-going tideway, did not seem the most sensible of ideas, and Stanley was ashore with the dinghy. Yo-yo swam across the bay, barking the while, and by the time Stanley returned in answer to my shouts he was out of sight and sound. I searched for an hour in the dinghy, and the next day we combed Wreck Bay and made enquiries far inland – all to no avail. Yo-yo had, I concluded, found a watery grave. Well, he was born and bred a sea-dog, and died in his element. Poor little Yo-yo! I never thought it possible that an animal could be missed so much.

On leaving Wreck Bay I got restricted permission to visit Floreana, Albemarle and Narborough Islands. At Post Office Bay, Floreana, the whalers who came round the Horn established a mail-box in the form of a cask, in which they posted letters for home, and which was cleared by any homeward-bound craft. It was still occasionally used by such as me. Narborough Island is the home of the giant iguana; I would have liked to meet one, but was destined to be disappointed. The island is the most desolate place I ever hope to see, brown and volcanic, the coastal ground being a vast plain of lava lumps. Assuredly it was not a place to get into trouble, and as the current was strongly against us landing, I altered course out to sea.

It was a sobering thought that the next passage would be the longest we would make on the entire voyage – 3,000-odd nautical miles or 3,400 'land' miles, as far almost as London to Pakistan, without sighting land and with little likelihood of sighting any other ship – 3,400 miles of nothing but sea.

During the day and night of June 19th, in calms and light airs, we were carried by the current. In the darkness the phosphorescent water was amazing. When the breeze was sufficient to carry us through the water, we left a path of shimmering silver in our wake. A friendly sea-lion followed us for over an hour, diving, surfacing, puffing and blowing out through his moustache. We could follow his movements clearly by his phosphorescent wake beneath the surface. A fine sailing breeze sprang up from the south-east at midnight, and carried us clear of the land.

Next day I got the ship to steer herself under all plain sail with the tiller lashed slightly a-weather. Thus trimmed she steered a fairly steady course with the wind abeam or just before the beam. Another method of self-steering, with the wind from the quarter or astern, was effected by rigging a line from the clew of the staysail, through a couple of leading blocks on the weather side, to the tiller, and a strong rubber band (actually the inner tube of a bicycle tyre!) from the tiller to the lee gunwale. Thus, if *Solace* started to turn to windward the wind pressure on the staysail would cause this line to pull the tiller to windward, and back she would go on course. If she started to turn *away* from the wind, the staysail would become slack and the bicycle tyre would pull the tiller over and bring her back on course. With careful adjustment, a pretty steady course could be maintained.

All that day, with a steady Force 3 breeze, she steered herself without any attention from the crew. For the first week at sea we continued under this rig on a south-south-west course, with the object of picking up the trade winds which blow with greater strength and reliability further south.

At this stage I started a system of 'routines'. On an extended passage things tend to get out of order without one being aware of it. I constantly came across rusty tins, mouldy books, seized-up winches and a score of other things, so I worked out a monthly timetable to ensure that one day clothes lockers would be aired, on another the bedding, on another that the winches would be oiled, and so on. That may sound more like naval routine than yachting, but in practice it is plain common sense. Casual supervision could have resulted in inefficiency, discomfort, waste, danger, and possibly ill-health.

I had not had a haircut for eight weeks, so after preliminary instructions I had one from Stanley. On completion he exclaimed with a beaming smile, 'You look like Rudolf Valentino!' At four-thirty that morning a breeze sprang up from the south-east and by daylight it was blowing a good Force 4, increasing to Force 5 at about midday. We had hit the trades at last.

With 2,500 miles to go, self-steering had to be brought into use on every possible occasion. We were now within a couple of degrees of the latitude of the Marquesas, and to continue on our present course with the wind before the beam would take us further south that I wanted to go. So we set a westerly course and again rigged the self-steering by staysail. We watched the results anxiously: *Solace* turned slowly round towards the wind, the tiller was hauled to windward by the straining staysail and back went the bow on to course, now beyond it – but over went the tiller, pulled to leeward by the rubber spring, and back she came on course again. Careful adjustments reduced the yawing by a few degrees and once more we were able to leave *Solace* to steer herself. But we kept a careful eye on her.

We found by experience that 'cabin watch' was essential. It meant that one of us, though free to wander about the ship or go below, must keep awake. No lying down. One soon got the 'feel' of the ship and if she started running off the wind and was in danger of gybing, as for no apparent reason she sometimes did, one could sense it and bring her back.

On the fourteenth day the wind backed to east, and we rigged twin staysails for a westerly course. The 'twins' were the most reliable method of self-steering which we used. They had no reefing arrangements, but were able to take anything up to Force 7. I found I could set the mizzen without interfering much with the steering, which gave us an extra three-quarters of a knot or so. We were not bound by the everlasting 'watch and watch' routine at the helm, and lived almost as in harbour, with both of us sleeping throughout the night. The big difference, of course, was the ship's motion: under this arrangement she rolled ceaselessly.

On the twenty-ninth day our first Polynesian visitor arrived, a frigate bird. On the thirty-third, an hour after sunrise, Stanley sighted the lofty eastern point of Hiva Oa dead ahead. We gave three cheers! Shortly afterwards, as the morning mist cleared, Motane and Fatu Huku appeared to port and starboard. It was on Hiva Oa that Paul Gauguin lived and died, but the anchorage looked unsatisfactory for a boat without an engine, and we decided to make for Nukuhiva, ninety miles away.

Early next morning skies were threatening everywhere. We swallowed a mug of hot cocoa and prepared for the worst. It came! – in a long series of the sharpest squalls I have ever encountered. They were led by a black squall hurling down buckets of rain which completely blotted out every trace of land and horizon. I watched with interest the belly in the sails, as one watches a balloon being blown up, nervously waiting for it to pop. I went forward and glanced up at the bending mast, which was so unpleasant that I did not look again! A brief lull and the next squall was upon us. We could see the water astern whipped up white by the fury of the oncoming wind. I put Stanley by the tiller and went forward, ready to drop the sails if necessary. The ship leapt ahead as the squall struck us. I could not raise my head to face the rain, which flew past almost horizontally. The waves were beaten flat, the surface of the water white with spume. I have seldom felt so thankful that my tackle was sound.

Off the harbour mouth of Tai-o-hae, we headed blindly for the entrance of the calm but squall-puckered waters. As we sailed up the magnificent harbour, the winds swept over the mountains and down the gullies, bouncing off the western heights – they were impossible to forecast. We watched the ruffle on the water and tried to be ready; even so we were caught napping. A squall caught us aback, swinging the mizzen right over and parting the sheet – after a passage of thirty-three days and 3,200 miles, almost the only accident within half a mile and ten minutes of anchoring!

Chapter 12

The haven of Tai-o-hae is a beautiful expanse of water, over a mile and a half long and three-quarters of a mile wide, lying in an amphitheatre of mountains which rise in places to over 2,000 feet. Covered with rich vegetation, intersected by valleys and ravines which discharge their bubbling streams on to its palm-fringed, golden shores, the whole presents a scene of grandeur and rugged beauty.

It is a sad comment on human relationships in the so-called Christian era that the population of the Marquesas was reduced from 16,000 (one authority states 60,000) to under 3,000 in 150 years of unhappy contact with the white man. Granted, the inhabitants were cannibals, whose favourite manly pastime was inter-tribal warfare, but cannibalism in itself does not signify decadence – merely lack of education. We are repelled at the thought of putting Granny in the pot. But so were they. They just cooked their enemies.

The history of the Marquesas is in many ways typical of the South Seas, though probably in no island group has it been worse. As one writer puts it:

> The group was a happy hunting ground for the whalers, traders, slavers ('blackbirders') and all the white scum of the South Seas. The native men were taught all vices from alcoholism to opium smoking. The women were debauched. European diseases, against which these island folk had bred no immunity, went through the villages like wildfire; in epidemic after epidemic the natives died in masses. It is the most tragic and sordid story of the South Pacific.

We had not long anchored before a canoe was seen approaching, paddled by natives, with a European, smartly dressed in whites, sitting in the stern. Hastily slipping on a clean shirt, and trying to recall a few words of schoolboy French, I greeted him with '*Bonjour, Monsieur. Monsieur le Commissionaire, n'est-ce pas?*'

My visitor replied 'No, I am the Doctor. But what excellent French you speak!' He was far too polite to point out to me that the French for Commissioner is *Commisseur* – *Commissionaire* meaning precisely the same in France as it does in England! That was my introduction to Dr Pierre Treac, and the interesting and happy time I had on lovely Nukuhiva was due almost entirely to him and his Swedish wife Karin.

They asked me whether I would like to ride over the mountains to one of the adjacent valleys before I left. Of course I would. But I was left in no doubt as to the risks. Wet weather would render it too dangerous. In order to tune up neglected riding muscles we had a couple of afternoons fence-jumping on the football field. After two rainless days the well-mounted convoy set out – Pierre, Karin, myself and Kuku, a young and powerfully built Marquesan, whom one would have imagined to have been born on a horse and who was the finest hunter in the islands.

On the lower slopes the track led through dense bush, occasionally crossing, or even following, the boulder-strewn bed of a river, but always going up, until we reached a clearing on the heights looking out to sea and over the magnificent bowl of Tai-o-hae harbour. The deep blue of the open sea was flecked with white horses, whipped up by the same fresh trade wind that was blowing round us as we watched from 1,500 feet or more, but within the horseshoe of sheltering mountains the water was calm as a mill-pond and *Solace* could be seen lying serenely on it, looking very small and seemingly almost touching the fringing reef.

Higher up, the track led us across open grassland, round the shoulders and over the tops of hills, then across a plateau of dense low scrub, to a ridge where sheep were grazing, and from which a truly awe-inspiring view presented itself. Immediately below us lay a deep valley running down to the sheltered cove of Hakatea. Beyond the valley lay ridge upon ridge, densely wooded, and in

81

the distance the 4,000-foot peak which caps the island.

But where did we go now? I glanced with undisguised horror at the precipitous slopes beneath us, then, like a lubber aloft taught not to look down, I followed closely on the heels of my companions, glueing my eyes to the narrow path. Several times the edge crumbled under the hoofs of the horse ahead of me, leaving a notch in the path as the bits of earth cascaded down below. Yet those steely-nerved creatures never hesitated and never slipped. I sweated freely until we reached the bottom of the valley and – Paradise!

Hakaui is, or was, a diminutive village in a sylvan setting on lush green grass, through which a crystal stream flows into the cove, craggy grey cliffs towering above it on either side, shutting out all but the noonday sun, which, in the tropics, is a blessing. There were few signs of civilization, or at any rate of those ugly elements such as corrugated iron roofs and noisy, smelly engines, which usually accompany it. We were refreshed, as is the Polynesian custom, with coconuts picked as we arrived. We walked up the valley to within sight of the waterfall, Vaipo, which though little more than a trickle in volume drops straight down a 2,000-foot cliff. What an eerie place it was! It could have been the inspiration for an Edgar Poe fantasy. In one place, at the edge of a shallow cave several hundred feet up the cliff face, was the tomb of a chieftain, buried there, apparently, to preserve his body from marauding tribes. To us the puzzle was how on earth they got him up there in the first place.

After a picnic lunch of grilled sausages, we were off on that giddy trail again. On the higher grassy slopes, Kuku would leave us now and then to chase an errant steer, and I watched admiringly his disregard of contour as he took the shortest routes, negotiating with ease slopes which I would never attempt. Kuku was a tough nut and I had made little headway in his affections, but on the return journey I found the key to his heart. We reached the end of the half-mile of sandy crescent foreshore; I said to him 'You like to race?' He looked surprised and smiled. I repeated the invitation, and off we set at a gallop. We both went flat out and finished a few yards from the rocks neck and neck. Kuku, grining with delight, was my friend. What a glorious day's ride it had been, and how completely mad!

I felt sorry for myself next day, sore and sunburnt, and the time had come to move on. After sixteen happy days we said good-bye to our kind friends and sailed away.

★ ★ ★

I very much wanted to visit the Tuamotu Archipelago between the Marquesas and Tahiti – an extensive group of coral atolls which had been inadequately surveyed and where the currents are strong and unpredictable. It is an area to which yachtsmen normally give a wide berth. When it came to entering the passages leading through the reefs into the lagoons, the *Admiralty Sailing Directions* were larded with words such as 'unpredictable' 'caution' and so on. 'There is usually a race, with eddies and whirlpools and exceptionally heavy seas.'

My particular interest was in Raroia, the island on which the *Kon-tiki* was wrecked. The lagoon entrance is narrow, and entry would involve a beat to windward. I had no engine. So I went on board three trading schooners that put in to Tai-o-hae and discussed it with their skippers. Two of them said 'No – don't try.' One said 'Yes'. My own private opinion was that I could.

In the following late afternoon we passed the island of Ua Pou, eight miles to the eastward, its spire-like mountains reflecting the light of the setting sun, impressive and unreal as in a Walt Disney fairy-tale film. What sort of subterranean convulsions had produced such a fantastic, topsy-turvy skyline?

It was grand sailing. The first forty-eight hours took us 222 miles – not exceptional, but good. I had timed our visit to Raroia so that we would arrive with the waxing moon and have the advantage of moonlit nights for navigating in this famously wreck-strewn area. My sole chart of the island was a large-scale one, showing only the passage into the lagoon and down to the village. I had no chart of the whole atoll to show me exactly where the passage was. When a passage through the reef did appear, it looked horribly narrow. The current was running through it at anything up to eight knots. I told Stanley to steer for the middle of the passage, and risked it.

Luckily the wind enabled us to head straight up through, and when the current caught us we swept in like a train. I was mesmerized by a snake-like strip of blue, indicating shallow water, that ran across in front of us. We're there, we're over, we're past – phew! we're between the two points of land. Now for some tricky, high-speed navigation. According to the chart, which I had memorized until it was like a photograph in my brain, I had 100 yards to go before turning into an S-bend through the coral rocks.

The all-important beacons were missing! Others had changed topmarks, one or two were new. All my forethought had been useless, and we were heading at eleven knots for a rock less than eighty yards away. I dashed up to the fo'c'sle and looked into the blue of the lagoon for a deeper blue which would indicate the channel, and gave signals to Stanley with my hand. We wound our way past and between the dark-brown patches which warned of coral rocks, missing some by inches, until, clear of the current, we were gliding quietly down towards the village.

The chief of Raroia, Tenghea, came off in a canoe to greet us, and helped us to a safe anchorage, fastening an anchor into one of the coral heads. That is the local method. They go right up to a coral head, which is rather like a mushroom in shape, the crew jumps on to it and places the anchor in a cleft.

We were soon the centre of interest of the population of 118. The *Kon-tiki* was still a lively memory on Raroia and there was a particular affection for Bengt Danielson, the Swede, who later returned to the island and lived there for a year. The folk who gathered round me explained that they were all his 'friends', and one was, in fact, his adopted 'father'. Tenghea paid us many visits during our stay and, despite a slight language difficulty, conversation and interest never seemed to flag. His interpreter was a pretty girl of about thirteen, named Piho, who had learned English on the yacht of William Robinson and his wife some two or three years previously.

He and other numerous visitors loved looking at my photographs. I raked up a Bond Street cabinet portrait of myself in uniform which created a terrific impression – possibly because of the contrast with the tousled, hirsute fellow they were talking to. They immediately asked if I were married, but if the question was a form of compliment it was quickly neutralized by Tenghea's candid comment that I look better without a beard – a particularly deflating remark as I had only trimmed it that morning.

Two urgent requirements on arriving in harbour were always freshwater bathing and laundry facilities. I asked Tenghea if we could have baths ashore, and he conducted us to the schoolhouse. Beside it was a large concrete tank, from the side of which protruded a tap, some three feet above the ground.

'You may bath here,' announced young Piho.

'Here?' I queried, thinking I must have misunderstood her.

'Yes,' she said, with a charming smile.

'But how do I get a bath here?' I asked.

'You sit down under the tap.' I repeated her words incredulously.

'Yes,' she beamed.

I glanced at the surrounding houses and the schoolhouse and thought of the entertainment I would provide. 'But – but what about . . . what about all these houses?'

'Oh, they won't mind! Chief says it is quite all right. I will come with you and turn the tap on, if you like.'

My reluctance to play the leading part in this popular local drama must have shown in my face, as, after a consultation with Tenghea, Piho said:

'Chief says it would be better for us to carry water to my father's house and you can use his bathroom.' I hastily agreed, reflecting at the same time that I was missing rather a unique ceremony.

The days passed pleasantly enough in what Bengt Danielson has christened 'The Happy Island'. I was anxious to see the tiny islet on the windward side of the lagoon, close to which the *Kon-tiki* was wrecked, and I invited Tenghea to take the tiller while I tended the sheets. But *Solace* is not a sailing canoe, and would not do as he wanted, and in a short time we were drifting down towards the reef. With my heart in my boots, I dropped the sails; this electrified the stout figure at the helm. In a stentorian voice he roared a brief order towards the shore, and in less time than it takes to recount, thirty to forty men, women and children had torn down the beach and across the reef. They reached the sharp, sheer edge simultaneously with *Solace* and in a line from stem to stern they threw their weight against her side and held her clear.

A dozen men jumped on board and there followed a scene of indescribable confusion. I had no idea what was happening, but before long I realised that everyone was doing a perfect job. Canoes were alongside, the second anchor and long warp were out, a diver down to make sure it held, and the ship hauled off clear of the reef. It cannot have been ten minutes before *Solace* was lying comfortably with her anchor on the same coral head as before.

Standing on deck, my feelings a mixture of intense relief, thankfulness and admiration, I became aware that Tenghea's interpreter was saying to me 'Chief says, shall we go to Kon-tiki now?' What a man!

We went, and as we approached the islet, I thought I had never seen anything so beautiful. It is not more than eighty yards across, but a perfect miniature of a coral island. Tenghea showed us the actual place where the raft had grounded, and the young coconut tree planted by the crew. Everyone then went fishing – the main preoccupation of all Polynesian islanders.

Return transport was according to taste. Piho's brother swam. Tenghea thought it was time he used our dinghy, and provided the entertainment of the day. Stanley rowed while the chief sat in the stern; the bow pointed to the skies, and there was never any hope of reaching the shore, but the boat remained in unstable equilibrium long enough to have the entire population at the pierhead in uncontrollable laughter, before submerging and leaving its occupants to swim for it.

In the meantime Piho had fallen for Stanley. Having no inhibitions on the subject, she had made that plain within twenty-four hours of arrival, giving him a look that would have melted a less susceptible heart than his. The course of true love had apparently run to form, and despite the full moon and romantic setting, Stanley had not co-operated very well. None the less, she persuaded her father to invite him to stay for good. He diplomatically, if rather dishonestly, postponed the issue by declaring that he would come back one day.

Our wonderful stay was concluded with a grand feast and a sad farewell, and we set forth under a fresh easterly breeze.

Chapter 13

I was still ready to meet further challenges in the Tuamotus, and decided on the atoll of Kauehi, described as 'very low and dangerous to approach at night'. At midnight we shortened sail and proceeded cautiously towards it. When day broke it was a battle to enter the lagoon, but it proved to be worth it: the shallow water was exceptionally varied in colour and very lovely.

A short week-end was all we could afford there, and when the time came to leave it was even harder to get out. We left on an out-going tide, wearing oilskins and sou'-westers, and with our hatches, skylight and scuttles firmly closed. The current caught us and rushed us through the passage, eddies swept and turned us this way and that, whilst Stanley heaved away at the tiller trying to keep us on course. I always put him on the helm when entering or leaving harbour, so that I could be free to take bearings and consult the chart. Now for the overfalls – crash! Over they came, solid green seas, gallons of water pouring over the upper deck and even the cabin top – a general gefuffle – and *Solace*, like a bull in a china shop, smashing her way through it regardless, the jib scooping up water as the bowsprit dipped into it, and even the bottom six feet of mainsail drenched with spray. Barely a minute, and it was all over, and, with water still streaming along the scuppers and dripping from our oilskins, we were gliding smoothly on.

We visited Rangiroa, at forty miles long the largest atoll in the group but, as was usual in the Tuamotus, the highest piece of ground was about seven feet above sea level, the tops of the trees about seventy feet. In striking contrast, the mountains of Tahiti are over 7,000. We sighted the peaks of Mounts Orohena and Aorai peeping above the clouds at a distance of exactly 100 miles.

We continued under self-steering, until we met the fringing reef, then coasted down until we spotted the passage into Papaeete lagoon.

Tahiti has been called the 'Pearl of the Pacific', and that it once justified the title is perhaps true. Literature has painted a picture of beauty, charm and romantic delight, and that the island possesses all these things it would be stupid to deny. However, I found that the trappings of civilization were the same there as in any other part of the world. There was no charm or romance in French bureaucracy; in the wharf and Customs shed which I found occupying a large part of the waterfront at Papaeete; in the roar and clatter of traffic from bicycles to the latest American cars, all kicking up dust and tooting their horns; in the smoky, crowded saloons and the blatant demi-monde community.

But if Papaeete did bring me down to earth with a shock, it was not without interest, with its European residences, British and French-owned shops and little Chinese emporiums in the back-streets. It was extraordinary what you could get in these shops. In the middle of the town was the big ugly market building, and if you went there early any morning you could get a good idea of who lived on Tahiti and what they grew. But we seldom had to go as far as the market for our requirements. Along the waterfront, within a few yards of us, were several little food stalls, open all day and late at night. Even after they closed, the vendors – usually consisting of an entire family – slept under or around their stalls, and we could usually still make an emergency purchase.

I enjoyed my stay in Papaeete, largely due to Freddie Devenish, the popular, unconventional British Consul, and to meeting two American writers, Jim and Susie McConnaughty, who owned a lovely bungalow, where I was able to enjoy the pleasantest of civilization's amenities in lazy, tropical surroundings. My drives with them around the island decided me to quit Papaeete and move *Solace* to one of the more pleasant anchorages at Papeari on the south coast. It was beautiful and peaceful, we made friends at the nearby village, and we were able to do some refitting work on board.

I had made up my mind to climb Mount Aorai, the second highest mountain in Tahiti, which had a recognized track kept in good order. It involved crossing a knife-edge ridge, but the view was breath-taking. I stayed the night up there in a hut thoughtfully provided with primus, kettle, cutlery and tinned food. The blankets were 'more holey than righteous' and I was aware of some astonishing variations in the weather, and at daybreak found myself enveloped in cloud. At one period there was an unearthly silence. You may find yourself nearer to God on the top of a mountain, even than at sea.

I have never been allowed to leave any place in the South Sea islands without being loaded with fruit and vegetables. As a rule, the smaller and more out-of-the-way the place, the more generous the people. We left Papeari with 400 bananas on board – amongst other things! It would have been pointless trying to dissuade the donors, who would have felt very hurt if I had not accepted them with every sign of pleasure.

The southern aspect of Tahiti from the sea, so seldom seen by anyone, is by far the most imposing – fifteen miles of thickly wooded slopes, deeply scored by over a dozen valleys running straight inland for three to six miles and up to heights of nearly 6,000 feet. The sun-kissed ridges, on the early morning as we left, alternating with the still shaded valleys, gave the picture a rippling appearance of rare beauty.

Our wanderings took us to Moorea, Bora-Bora, Maupiti and other lovely islands which cannot be accommodated in this short account. We spent six delightful days in Rarotonga, and intended to go on to Samoa, calling en route at Palmerston Island on the western outskirts of the Cook group. Palmerston atoll is 260 miles north-west from Rarotonga, and a wind from the south-east rolled us along under stay-sails at a leisurely pace. The sky was mottled with tufts of cloud like pieces of cotton wool – which is sometimes referred to as a 'trade-wind' sky.

The second morning out, the sky clouded over and midday found us waddling along in a light breeze. This was unfortunate, as I expected to sight Palmerston the next morning. It is barely five miles wide and, like all atolls, so low-lying that it cannot be seen at a distance of more than eleven or twelve miles even on the clearest day. There is also a considerable ocean current in this area, and moreover I had not fixed my position for a full day and a half. At nightfall there was not a star to be seen. To make matters worse, going on deck at dawn I found that instead of steering north-west we were heading north-north-east, the wind having shifted, heaven alone knows when, whilst we were asleep. But my luck was in – the stars were out and I was able to take sights. We set course once again for Palmerston and four hours later a low line of coconut palms could be seen stretching out on our port bow.

At about four o'clock a sail was sighted rounding one of the islets on the reef. We closed it and hove to. In the boat were ten men, as motley a collection as you could find anywhere, all colours from white to dark brown, all bare-footed, some with hats, some without, some in shorts, some in longs, all except one in a variety of shirts, vests or jackets, the exception being so hairy on arms, chest and back that he scarcely needed any other protection. Two of them stepped on board *Solace* and greeted us in English, introducing themselves as Ned and Tom Marsters.

The story of the Marsters family is well known in the Pacific, often with inaccuracies and exaggerations. This, briefly, is how it was told to me on Palmerston Island.

William Marsters was born in Birmingham in 1821 and ran away to sea as a cabin boy at the age of fourteen. He joined the whalers and eventually became a mate. In 1850 he jumped ship at Penrhyn Island in the Northern Cooks. After numerous adventures he found himself with three native wives and the ownership of Palmerston Island. In due course a family was produced by each of the wives, and by the time of my visit William's descendants, now in the fifth generation, numbered over a thousand, scattered through the Cook Islands and New Zealand.

In spite of his sins, old William seems to have brought up his family strictly and on sound commonsense lines. The boys were frequently made to row to the other side of the lagoon and back

– nine miles – before breakfast, and learned to hunt and fish, build houses and a score of other crafts before they were in their 'teens. They were also taught to read their Bible and 'make prayer' morning and evening.

The oft-repeated story of in-breeding on Palmerston with astonishingly healthy results is a myth. Marriage between brother and sister was forbidden. Half-brothers and sisters were allowed to marry, but in fact only one couple did so. The rest took Maori husbands and wives from other islands, and healthy their descendants certainly are.

William Marsters would not allow his children to speak anything but English, and it was only in the previous three generations that they had learned to speak Maori, but the latter language was never used on Palmerston in conversation. Their isolation and the passage of time had produced a 'basic basic English' of quaint character and rustic accent, perhaps handed down from old William. On the whole their talk was easy to follow, and I found that provided I used simple words I was understood by them.

From 1899, when old William died, his eldest son, also William, ruled the island until 1946. Since his death in that year, Ned had been chief. Such, briefly, had been the history of Palmerston Island, where I intended to spend a long week-end.

We anchored on the western side of the atoll close off the reef and near to a boat passage. Ned Marsters then suggested I should come ashore with Stanley, have lunch and see the island. Under a scorching sun and with a south-east wind blowing across the lagoon and *Solace* anchored in smooth water under the lee of the reef, with a rich blue sea beneath us and a cloudless sky overhead, we looked across the reef with its foaming breakers to a lagoon of brilliant sapphire. Scattered round the reef were little islets, each a clump of fresh verdure with its coconut trees and green bushes. This, if it existed at all, must surely be the coral island of the story-books!

We jumped into their boat and were rowed inshore. Despite the calm sea, rollers were piling up one after another, arching their crests and breaking with a thunderous roar on the reef. Fifty yards outside the boat passage, the rowers rested on their oars and waited until the 'ninth great wave' had passed under us and broken, then bent to their oars and made a dash for it. Before the next big wave arrived we were in the passage. The tide was on the ebb, and the lagoon waters were rushing out at terrific speed. The oars were reinforced by paddles and in places a long pole. It had been twenty-five minutes hard rowing before we grounded on a beach of almost pure-white sand and were being carried ashore on lusty brown shoulders.

Palmerston is an atoll roughly trapezoid in shape. The reef, which is covered at high water and dry at low, has six main islets on it and a number of tiny ones. Of the main islets only one was inhabited, the others being visited for wood, coconuts, fishing and so on. As I stepped ashore I felt that here was the perfect paradise. Here was no overcrowding, but well-separated buildings, some of thatch, some of wood, each with its small detached cookhouse, lavatory and fenced washplace, its chicken run and pigsty, its well, perhaps too a small workshop and maybe a flower bed. Here and there was a fine breadfruit tree, a pawpaw, a few banana trees, a lime bush, and everywhere over all the forest of coconut trees providing shade as well as food and drink. Everywhere seemed clean, tidy and fresh.

In the centre of the island, in low-lying ground were the vegetable patches where, over two to three acres, tons of coral had been laboriously dug away until water was reached, and the pit filled with earth, rotting vegetable matter, sawdust and anything else which would form soil. We were shown the 'refuge hill', rising to about twenty feet above sea level, which enabled the islanders to survive when Palmerston was swept by hurricanes. On our way back to the Mission House we were shown a little wireless station with an old wartime set, by which the islanders communicated three times a day with Rarotonga. Ned pointed out the church, built from an old wreck, and entertained us on the verandah of the Mission House, one of only two houses on the island built in European bungalow style. After lunch a couple of boatloads of islanders went out to *Solace*, and we spent the rest of the afternoon showing them over the ship.

Next morning, Sunday, a canoe arrived to take me ashore. I left Stanley on board, intending to relieve him later on, but Ned offered to send someone on board as ship-keeper, to enable Stanley to join me, and to this I agreed. At about 8.30 we attended morning service, which Ned took in front of the whole population from a lofty pulpit with 'ZION' inscribed on the front. Sunday on Palmerston, as in many other parts of the world, was a fashion parade. Men and women turned out in their brightest colours, and it would have been hard to say which were the most colourful. To my European eyes the male attire was the more striking. One young buck sported a brilliant green pair of pyjamas with golden snakes and dragons on front and back.

Lunch at the Mission House was followed by the ringing of the bell (also from a wrecked ship) for the afternoon service. As I came out, Stanley, who had been sitting near the door, was making unintelligible signs to me, and on joining me said 'She's broke.' He pointed to seaward, where *Solace* was sailing under staysail and mizzen close to the reef. It turned out that the grapnel had slipped off the Japanese coral anchor, which was being used for the first time. Nobody seemed in the least concerned, Ned merely remarking that two of the boys would go out in a canoe and help the ship-keeper re-anchor her. I sent Stanley out with them, and soon *Solace* was re-anchored with the main anchor and chain. Ned offered us beds for the night; however I felt happier on board, so returned with Stanley after dark.

When we turned in, *Solace* was lying comfortably with her bows pointing towards the reef. At about eleven-thirty I woke up, feeling a pitching motion and aware of the sound of breakers from abaft the starboard beam. I went on deck and found that the wind had backed ten points or so and the ship had swung round towards the reef. A nasty sea had already got up and the taut cable was being subjected to a terrific strain every time the bows rose to the sea. The deck planking under the cable winch was actually lifting.

It was pitch dark, raining, and the anchor chain was clearly foul of a rock and liable to part at any moment. The first essential was to ease the strain on the cable; as we took the brake off, it flew out at such a rate that when I put it on again the spindle bent under the strain. The winch was then useless. The ship was pitching like a rocking horse, and eventually the cable parted. There was now no hope. We lay broadside on to wind and sea and we were already being lifted by the seas rearing their crests before breaking on the reef. It was a matter of seconds. I sent Stanley below for the lifebelts and we had scarcely put them on when the keel (thank God it was an iron one!) struck with a jarring shock. We clung to the rigging, smothered by the seas, as the ship was hurled onto the reef. Mercifully it was the top of high water, and a great wave lifted us clear of the reef-edge and flung us on top.

Unable to see anything but a maelstrom of black and white, our voices inaudible in the thunder of surf, we clung to the rigging, whilst wave after wave charged down upon us, smothering us with foam and flogging *Solace* further and further onto the reef. Fifty or sixty yards from the edge she lay on her beam ends while the seas continued to batter her.

During the next six hours the tide fell, and when it became possible we moved to the cabin, which by now looked like a ship-chandler's shop after a bomb-burst. The water was up to and into the wireless set. However, the gimballed table was at a correct, if not a normal angle, and the kettle was still sitting on the gimballed primus! I took the hint, and, with nothing else to do, we cheered ourselves up with copious cups of cocoa.

It was barely light when we saw the islanders coming out to us, some in canoes, some over the reef, Ned amongst them. There were a lot of long faces but little was said. The ship was obviously holed. I think I'm a born optimist, but my heart has never been nearer my boots than it was at that moment.

Chapter 14

Solace looked so small in relation to the reef around her, and yet so vast as she lay high and dry, that the mere thought of rescuing her seemed ludicrous. I remember saying, rather hopelessly, to Ned, 'Do you think we can save her?' – and his calm and unexpected reply: 'We'll try.'

If I had known him as well then as I did later on, I should have known that this meant, 'We'll do it.' As it was, the mere suggestion that salvage was possible acted as a spur on my spirits. I discussed ways and means with Ned, who seemed hopeful of hauling *Solace* over the quarter of a mile of reef to the lagoon, getting her afloat, and then towing her to an islet and beaching her. I had lost two anchors and half my chain, but I still had one heavy anchor and about fifteen fathoms of chain, the four three-inch warps that had brought me throught the Panama Canal, four double iron blocks and a lot of heavy shackles.

Almost every house on Palmerston had masses of junk stowed away, overhead, beneath the floorboards, or both, originally salvaged from some wreck or other, and a truly astonishing assortment of gear was dragged out and carted in canoes to the reef, and as the tide came in coconut rollers were being floated out until the place looked like a timber mill.

Every movable thing was lifted out of the ship and carried to the canoes. Ned put an empty house at my disposal for stowing the gear, and our personal things were taken to the Mission House. Everything washable was dealt with by the womenfolk. We then rigged the hauling gear. *Solace* was already pointing towards the lagoon, so we planted an anchor in a suitable hole in the coral rock, rigged chains and tackles to the mainmast and sampson post, placed logs under the bows, and started to haul. It was heavy going. By dusk we had moved her the best part of one and a half ship's length. We left the anchor and hauling gear rigged for the night and went ashore.

I was able to use the antiquated wireless set to send a message home and also report the disaster to Mr Nevill, the Resident Commissioner at Raratonga. He in his reply held out no hope of any ship calling in the near future. So there we were, marooned for at least nine months. All right – 'Let battle commence!'

During the next four weeks every able man and boy on the island, of whom there were seventeen all told, worked on the reef every day except Sunday. For the first three days the weather was filthy. When the gale had passed, the sun beat down and I personally suffered agonies from burnt skin and lips. My legs and ankles became covered in coral cuts, which invariably went septic and frequently turned into ulcers. I still have about a dozen scars.

The starboard side of *Solace* proved to be badly smashed in. Her bilges were filled with coral stones which washed in at high water and had continually to be cleared out. We lashed some forty-four-gallon drums under bow and stern to give her buoyancy, and re-rigged the hauling chain round her keel. A lot of coral heads had to be broken up with crowbars to clear her a passage. Meanwhile the coral heads to which we attached the chain kept breaking. On the 26th November we made a record haul – fifty-six yards. On the 7th December we lashed baulks of timber, a small tree and a canoe to the ship, and as the tide rose we started hauling. She came very slowly ahead, heeled over and dragging her keel. I sent four boys to the top of the mast to heel her further over, and the keel lifted clear. The hauling parties moved her by canoe, or by swimming from one coral head to another, and we beached and moored her an hour before dark.

It was on the twenty-second day after being wrecked that, with every man, woman and child on the ropes, we hauled *Solace* over heavy wooden planks placed in the sand into her berth under the coconut trees. What was left of the starboard side was so battered that the main shroud-plates had virtually no support, and raising her into an upright position presented some difficulty. We rigged tackles from coconut trees, and chocked her up with timber props and oil drums.

By now my helpers might with good excuse have wanted a rest, but no sooner was *Solace* securely fixed on an even keel than they set about removing the engine, freshwater tanks and furniture, and cutting away the wreckage. We were now able to make a thorough examination. There was a gaping hole for a length of eighteen feet between the two masts, and from about a foot below the deck to a foot above the keel – about five feet. The decks were in a bad way, the taffrail was broken and there was other damage, including to the water and electricity supplies. However, I realised how lucky I was that most absolutely vital parts: masts, rudder etc., were unharmed.

Every man on Palmerston Island well understood the principles of boat-building. Ned declared that the replacement of timbers would present no difficulty: he would fell a couple of mahogany trees. These were few and precious, and I felt immensely grateful. They were carried to the village sawpit, and we spent much time and sweat 'ripping them up'. But it was all good fun – nothing was ever done without lots of talk, leg-pulling and laughter. A thatch roof was built over the ship, a bench constructed down the starboard side, and work proceeded in all weathers. We took careful patterns from the outside of the hull on the port side and checked with careful measurements inside. After the new timber had been left to season for some time, the new frames were sawn and added to the patterns.

The foremanship was gradually assumed by Tuakana, Ned's son, a skilful and conscientious carpenter. During ten months of rebuilding, Tuakana and his faithful pal Kori never left the job. He kept me fully acquainted with everything he did, and I had the utmost confidence in him. Knowing what was put into the work, I never subsequently had any doubts as to its solidity and its ability to stand up to any test.

While rebuilding proceeded Stanley and I had ample opportunity of entering into the many-sided life of the islanders. I shall never cease to marvel at my good fortune in getting wrecked on

Palmerston. If I had wanted to get wrecked and had had the whole world to choose from I could not have found a better place! Green waving palm trees, white sandy beaches trimmed with verdant bushes, blue lagoon, cooled by the trade wind, no machinery (except for the tiny charging motor for the W/T batteries), no noises other than nature's, wholesome food in abundance, adequate physical exercise, plenty of boats and canoes for poling, paddling, rowing or sailing, English-speaking inhabitants, first-class boatmen and skilled carpenters and boat-builders. Robinson Crusoe did not do nearly so well!

The principal activity of the menfolk was fishing, and they had various methods of catching the fish which abounded both inside and outside the lagoon. Fishing with a spear is an art which I would like to have acquired, but I think years of practice would be needed before you could spear a fish at will. Sometimes when working on *Solace* Tuakana would suddenly say 'I'm going on the reef now. The tide's right', and I would accompany him. Off he would bound at the double, his broad, bare, leatherlike feet carrying his bulky form over the rough, sharp coral as fast as I could move on tarmac. It was hopeless, in fact crazy, to try and keep up, even in shoes. He would throw his spear, perhaps miss, grab it again and continue the chase. The chances were about even. Green fish and parrot fish were good eating – thick, soft, white flesh which melted in your mouth, and no bones!

Sailing races were always fun. There were usually about six boats competing. The course, as often as not, was a triangular one, taking them first to windward through a regular maze of coral heads, past a large one known as Cape Horn, to Tom's Islet, on reaching which one of the crew had to jump out, dash ashore, and plant a stick in the sand. Then on to the second rock known as Kick-me-arse, then home. Correct Rule of the Road was observed. After my first race I was overcome with curiosity over the name of that rock, and I asked Ned.

'Oh-h-h! dat,' he said. 'Dat was de name gi'en to it by our gran'father. 'E were beatin' up to it one day and de wind kep' on 'eadin' 'im off so's 'e couldna' make it, not fer long time. When 'e gets pass it 'e looks back and says, 'Now you can kick me arse!' An' dat's 'ow we use to call it ever since! An' dat's better'n some of de names 'e call it before 'e got round it, so my fader tell me!'

Little Palmerston Island became world news one day in March 1955. Over the radio to Rarotonga I had asked for some much needed supplies, and Mr Nevill had kindly made arrangements for the New Zealand W/T calibration aircraft to drop them for us. On the 21st it came zooming over, and down came two large mail bags. We watched aghast as the parachutes failed to open and the bags landed with a great thud in the sand. On opening them we found a large tin of glue and four tins of cement burst open, with consequences best left to the imagination. By the time we had sorted out the contents – copper nails and washers, twine, bent cooking utensils, letters, papers and so-on, all covered with glue and cement, we were so gummed up ourselves that our hands were more like turtles' flippers than anything else. But most things were de-gummed in due course, and the home mail was doubly welcome. We greatly appreciated this very special, helpful and in fact vitally necessary operation.

Marooned in mid-Pacific with scarcely a stitch of clothing to my name, I found in the mail-bag a letter from Messrs Gieves, the naval tailors of Bond Street!

Sir,

I am glad to tell you that we can still supply a real Gieves suit for about £30-£32 including purchase tax . . . if you need a new suit . . . call in and see them and us for yourself.

I am, sir,

Yours obediently for GIEVES LIMITED

If there is one thing guaranteed to make news it is an air drop to shipwrecked mariners. Immediately after it occurred I was contacted on the radio by the Press and asked for a story, which I sent. I was not prepared, all the same, for the headlines splashed across the pages of the national and provincial Press all over England and the Commonwealth within forty-eight hours:

'*Roamer's Lonely Pacific Paradise*', '*Life on coral atoll idyllic*' – says *Crusoe*, and so on.

I could scarcely have stayed on Palmerston for so long without contributing something to the islanders' life, and they were quick to show the ways in which I could help them. It was within ten days of being wrecked that I was asked to give instruction in the use of the sextant. This developed into a navigation class covering coastal and deep-sea navigation, chart work, the use of the compass and sextant, the use of navigation tables, star recognition, and rounding off ultimately with a 500-mile voyage for practical application.

Later on, finding that the standard of reading was low, either Stanley or I took on an advanced class of schoolchildren at reading five afternoons a week, when other work permitted.

Very early on I was roped in on a somewhat different line. On my first Sunday, Tuakana had asked me if I knew any Bible stories I could tell them. I said, 'Yes, I think I can', and in my simplest English told one, and then another. Later in the evening Tuakana said 'the boys' wanted some more. These were half a dozen lads in their late 'teens and early twenties and with the help of a Bible I told them four or five stories. This became a routine every Sunday, developing in time into a quiz session and then a small study group.

The next request rather shook me. The church services were normally taken in turn by five 'deacons' – all Marsters, of course, and I was asked if I could help prepare sermons! During my stay on Palmerson I eventually prepared over sixty sermons, which were written down and deposited with Tuakana. Nor did things rest there. I was invited to instruct the Boys' Brigade and the Sunday School. In the latter, the small children seldom understood a word of what I was saying. The only answer was to start a Mothers' Meeting! All mothers, grannies, aunts and elder sisters would assemble for a Bible story from me in simple English. They would then go home and tell it in their own way to their children.

Hymns were also in great demand and I did manage, with the help of Annie, the schoolteacher, to teach the children several hymns, modified here and there to suit tropical conditions, which became very popular. I did the conducting while Annie led the singing, keeping it going and keeping order at the same time with a stick. It went something like this:

'Little children all should be (*whack!*)
Mild (*whack!*), obedient (*whack!*), good as –

Taia, if you don't wake up I come to you! – BILL! (*whack!*) –'

From this it will be gathered that Palmerston folk, besides being remarkably tough, talented and kind-hearted, were also very religious.

Time passed all too quickly, and when a schooner arrived, nine months after the shipwreck, *Solace* was well on the way to completion.

Chapter 15

The schooner brought Joaba Marsters, a nephew of Ned's, who had the reputation of being one of the best boat-builders on the island, so that Tuakana, who had borne the brunt of the work, had now first-rate assistance during the last few weeks. By the schooner also came supplies from New Zealand, furnished very trustingly by Messrs John Burns of Auckland. It is only fair to say that if no stores had arrived I firmly believe Tuakana would have finished the job. The resourcefulness and ingenuity of the islanders was amazing. One day I asked Ned if he had a very small paintbrush for *Solace*'s name letters. He went outside brandishing a large pair of scissors.

'Eddie!' – calling to an eight-year-old grandson – 'Come 'ere. Come and 'ave yer 'ead chopped off!'

It was the work of a moment to snip off Eddie's forelock, cut and trim a twig, and bind on the hair with a thread.

The only timber available for planking up the side was some from an old wreck. We selected the best, and every rusty and rotten bit – they ran into scores – was cut out and the planks plugged with good pieces until the requisite lengths of sound planking were obtained.

Solace was now ready for launching. Her 'coconut hat' was removed, and she was levered round until she was facing the lagoon, where an anchor with a length of chain was placed on a coral head. Another chain was rove round the keel, and a tackle rigged between the two. She was hauled out on log rollers, and two half-days' work saw her afloat. The final problem was to get her out of the lagoon; we put back nothing into her which could reasonably be spared until she was over the reef. One day at high water we kedged her down wind from coral head to coral head, her keel bumping occasionally, into the deep water in one of the boat passages. There she was turned and held by warps whilst the staysail was set and we sailed her out. We anchored her in exactly the same spot as nine and a half months before. Everyone was beaming with pride and delight.

It was now October, with nearly two months to go before the hurricane season, so I decided to make a trial run to Rarotonga and back, combining it with a practice cruise for my navigating class. On our successful return, I offered to take passengers, Kori and another keen lad called Tuatai, to New Zealand and bring them back on completion of *Solace*'s final refit, for which I had been recommended to go to Mr Bert Woollacott, an elderly retired boat-builder and designer.

The side planking put on *Solace* in Palmerston was ripped off and Mr Woollacott, a very good-natured old gentleman with white hair and apple cheeks, made a close inspection of the frames and pronounced an emphatic verdict: 'Don't you touch them. You won't get as good a job as that done anywhere in New Zealand!' So we got on with planking up the side with new timber. The deck canvas had to be renewed, a tricky and laborious job, and a new motor was installed, rigging refitted, and the ship finally spruced up.

Nine months had gone by since our arrival in Auckland, during which Stanley, Tuatai and I had made many friends (Kori had returned to the Cook Islands). September 15th saw us sailing away to a typical New Zealand farewell – much waving of scarves and handkerchiefs, tooting of horns, and a particularly loud cheer (or should I say jeer?) when we hoisted our jib upside down. There was of course only one possible place to go – Palmerston. Quite apart from an almost irresistible pull on the heartstrings, which will continue to my dying day, there were many practical reasons to go thither.

Solace's waterline had twice had to be cut in afresh – higher up! – since I had acquired her. The extra equipment and weight of stores essential for extended ocean cruising had made it necessary in the West Indies. In Auckland we had topped up our sea stocks, and in addition had embarked a large quantity of stuff for

Palmerston, so that the waterline was completely submerged. The freeboard amidships was a mere nineteen inches, and if Mr Plimsoll had had any say in the matter I fear we should not have sailed at all.

After a few hours, we came in for a blow. Bad weather in a small boat can be very trying to the temper. The motion of the boat produces a drain of energy which goes on twenty-four hours a day, the muscles are never at rest, and at night one is condemned to a sort of semi-sleep which cannot possibly restore one's strength. On every passage Stanley and I both lost pounds of weight. In my case, there was also the nervous strain of being in a state of subconscious awareness of what was happening, which can never be safely discarded at sea. This passage was more trying than most. An extra man in the crew meant a sharing of work, but also less room. Every available bit of space below deck was now encumbered with baggage of all sorts. To get something from forward was like a mountaineering expedition.

On the 1st October/30th September (we recrossed the dateline, at 4am) Tuatai was at the helm, and I was woken by a jarring shock. 'Great Scott! We've gone aground! No, impossible. What was that, Tuatai?'

'We jus' run over a whale,' said Tuatai, in a voice completely devoid of emotion. Gazing into the darkness astern we could see Moby Dick blowing a jet of white water – possibly a mild protest. He had bent the iron stem fitting for the bobstay, but he could certainly have smashed us like an eggshell with a flick of his tail.

We received a warm and happy welcome on return to Palmerston and it was only the realisation of our approaching final departure that clouded our enjoyment of a further spell of life on the island. Ned Marsters had persuaded me to stay over the first week-end in June of the following year, to 'eat bosun' with him. As bosun bird is *the* delicacy on Palmerston, this was a compliment I could not disregard. Over the last few days, when so many things were done for the last time, there was an unmistakable air of sadness which left us in no doubt that our friends regretted our coming departure as much as we did.

On the day of our departure, Ned gathered the whole island on the beach. We sat in a semi-circle under the palm trees facing the lagoon, and in a most moving ceremony Ned spoke a few words, after which the islanders all sang a Maori hymn in beautiful harmony. Ned then 'made prayer' for us and our voyage, closing with Psalm 121 and reading verse 8 as 'thy going away and thy coming back'. Dear old Ned! I am not ashamed to own that my eyes were more than misty. Stanley and I had to kiss over eighty people, nearly all of them in tears, and as I embarked in the loaded boat waiting to take us off, I was in much the same state myself. As we sailed away for Tonga, we watched them do as we had together so often done – row into the reef passage, tow their boat through the race, and sail across to the island. They had just reached the shore when a point of land hid them from our view.*

★ ★ ★

The Tonga islands at that time were seldom visited by yachts. The area is studded with reefs and islands, some coral, others volcanic, with frequent earth tremors. My risks, however, were calculated. The more dangerous the area, the more careful I always was to provide myself with the largest-scale charts and study them thoroughly. Slap-happy methods in coral waters are inexcusable.

I found that Western civilization had been impressing itself on the villages of the Tongan islands, where the houses were being built of corrugated iron instead of thatch, but we were shown traditional hospitality and on one occasion on Vava'u treated to some truly magnificent singing, entirely unaccompanied. I consider Tongans to have the finest voices in the Pacific. The women's voices are vibrant and rich, the men's deep and sonorous.

From Tonga we went on to Samoa, where I visited Vailima – the house of Robert Louis Stevenson – , and then Fiji. Here we witnessed fire-walking, which was actually a religious healing ceremony, all the performers being sufferers from some illness or other which the rites were supposed to cure. They danced themselves into a frenzy, at which point the priest drove skewer-like

* I am still in touch by correspondence with Tuakana.

106

instruments into their flesh – right through both cheeks, through lips, tongue, shoulder-muscles and other parts. Thus adorned and disfigured, they went in procession to the fire pit with bare feet.

The fire was a red-hot pile of ash and embers, which, I was told, had been burning for two days. Sitting during the performance fifteen yards away, I could feel the heat. A lady went into the temple afterwards and was allowed to examine the performers' feet, which she said were neither burned nor blistered.

Much as I would have liked to dally amongst the hundreds of islands of Fiji, the season was well advanced and I had to move on. I had been greatly interested in what I had read of the New Hebrides, some 500 miles west. They were one of the least civilized in the South Seas, and probably therefore the least spoiled in some ways. I could not resist visiting an area where two villages on one island often spoke entirely different languages, and where even cannibalism had not been entirely eradicated. We put into Lenakel, on the island of Tanna, where we came in for more excitement than we had bargained for.

Local legend says that the god of the volcano threw down stones which bore the secret of wisdom and prosperity, but that the white man pinched them all. Since 1941 there had been a particular 'cargo cult' on Tanna – the cult of 'Jon Frum', which had acquired such a grip that the Mission flocks had been decimated and the Administration had become rather worried. Jon Frum was a mythical American Negro who, the natives said, would one day come in a white ship, leading a convoy of ships laden with all the wonderful things which the white man enjoys.

On a certain Sunday there had been celebrations in the villages, at which the leaders had said that Jon Frum would arrive at the end of the week. The following Saturday night, after dark, a white ship was seen to glide silently into Lenakel anchorage and drop anchor – *Solace*! The British Resident Agent and the doctor came off in a canoe to tell me that the place was buzzing with excitement and that I must prepare to be crowned 'Messiah' shortly. But next morning, when a local man called Louhman came on board, he, after a hesitant glance at me, bowed to Stanley and endeavoured to explain that, as their long-awaited Messiah, a great welcome awaited him ashore. Stanley appealed to me.

'Nothing to do with me, old boy! Over to you!' I replied. 'You'd best put on your best bib and tucker and go ashore.' Subsequent events are best described as recorded by Stanley.

'It isn't every day that one gets an opportunity of being mistaken for a Messiah. At Tanna such an opportunity knocked at my door. The natives of Tanna believe that a Messiah called Jon Frum will come and deliver them from the rule of the white man. By some very strange coincidence Jon Frum was due to arrive on the day I did. It was only natural that they should think I was He. Louhman, their leader, who spoke a little English, welcomed me with deference. The other natives kept at a respectful distance from my divine person. When Louhman asked if I was Jon Frum and received a negative reply, he merely thought I was being modest. He proceeded to outline his case, the gist of which was that his people did not want to be ruled by the white man. Louhman sought my advice. I decided that I would have to be careful, as my answers could have far-reaching effects, so I advocated patience and trust in God. Louhman seemed quite pleased with my counsel. We talked of many things, my listeners hanging on my lips. When I tell you that during my five-day stay at Tanna I consumed no less than seven chickens, roast pig, and the very best of everything, you'll get an idea of what it's like to be a Messiah!'

The villagers feasted Stanley almost to bursting point, and talked of Jon Frum until he was bored stiff.

On 24th August we set sail for Papua, 1,200 miles to the north-west. On the way, we stopped at the little island of Kwato, just off the southern tip of the peninsula, where we were welcomed at the Mission House by a friend of mine, Russell Abel, and his wife Sheila. *Solace* needed to be hauled ashore and given a scrub and a coat of paint, and this was done in their boatyard. Here I heard from the skipper of a pearling lugger that conditions in the Torres

Strait, the Gulf of Carpentaria and the Timor Sea were quite hopeless for a sailing vessel. I had missed the last of the trade winds in those parts. All my instincts revolted at the notion of using the engine, besides which we should have been in a nice mess if it broke down, since I had not a hope of being able to mend it.

Russell was an expert on Papua, with its infinite variety of scenery, people and customs, and the next six months were truly happy and interesting. Part of the time I spent skippering a river boat for the London Missionary Society some 300 miles up the coast. Time flew by, and Mid-April arrived with the first signs of the returning trade wind. After two busy weeks of preparing for sea – in which we were greatly helped by our friends – we sadly bade farewell.

Chapter 16

To glance at a map of Torres Strait is to give yourself nightmares. A large-scale map helps you to breathe a little more freely, though you realise there is no room for taking chances. There was no up-to-date information on lights, so we were compelled to confine our sailing to daylight hours.

The 1,600-odd miles from Torres Strait to Bali, which took us twenty-two days, shall be dismissed in a few sentences. There is nothing more irritating to the sailing man than light airs and calms. The constant banging of booms, slatting of windless sails and rattling of blocks wear out the gear, and the racket down below is equally wearing to the temper. Until we were past the south-west tip of Timor, we never had more than a Force 3 breeze.

However, we were able to run under self-steering, and I used my free time brushing up the Malay I had learned during the war. Stanley was roped in to test the fluency of my vocabulary and idiom. He did all the navigating, taking morning and evening star sights every day, and concentrated on his study of seamanship, navigation and signal manuals. I gave him semaphore and morse exercises. We both did a lot of reading. But the mind cannot absorb more than the seat can endure; my diary for one day reads: 'Lay on deck in late afternoon and sunned my bottom, which is getting sore from sitting down.'

On May 29th we sailed into Benoa at the southern end of Bali and anchored in its landlocked harbour.

My memories of Bali deserve a book to themselves. Surely in the whole world there is not so much artistic talent in so small a compass. Everyone seemed to be an artist, and I mean everyone. The man who played one of the gongs in the gamelan orchestra might have driven me in a taxi that afternoon; another one playing beside him might have been a policeman. The leader of one such orchestra was of the princely caste. The man whose paintings I bought owned a small grocery store. Some of the loveliest carving in wood and bone was the handiwork of peasants. Exquisite silverwork was being done by schoolboys. The most wonderful dancing I saw was performed by a little girl of eight.

The Balinese co-operative way of life permits ample leisure, and there is a remarkable community spirit. Private enterprise seems to have no part in the true island economy. It is a system of exchange of goods and services which to all appearances brings an unparalleled degree of happiness and good fellowship.

Most of my visit was spent with Dr and Mrs Spencer Reid. We had mutual friends at home, and the doctor also had some ocean-cruising experience. He was running an anti-leprosy campaign covering the whole of Bali, and several days a week he motored to different parts of the island, taking me with him. He had to visit 1,200 patients at sixty-eight widely scattered centres, so his method of travel was rather like a racing motorist when in the car and an American tourist when out of it, but I did see a good deal.

Bali's main product is rice; we seemed, therefore, to be for ever passing through a sea of the most lush green imaginable. Even the hillsides were terraced for planting paddy. The villages were almost always in the shelter of trees, the houses in mud-wall compounds carefully designed to keep the spirits out, each family compound having its own group of shrines. Conspicuous in each village were the Hindu temples enclosing pagoda-like shrines, their gates and walls ornately decorated with friezes. Propitiating evil spirits is an important part of Balinese life. I suppose the fact that people do not live in constant dread is because they have complete confidence in their methods of propitiation.

One evening, in the romantic setting of the Jekorde's palace courtyard, we watched the performance of a *baris*, a pantomime based on one of the ancient myths, in which masked figures do considerably more talking than acting, with singing and dancing, accompanied in this case by a thirty-six-piece gamelan orchestra. The spectators knew the story by heart and provided an audience

111

such as all actors pray for, reacting visibly and audibly by laughing, growling, gasping, recoiling, some children even crying with fright, and never for a moment relaxing their attention.

It was at the palace, too, that I used to go and watch the *legong* being practised in an outer courtyard. I found it more entrancing each time I saw it. One of the oldest Balinese dances, it is performed by girls between seven and fourteen years of age. At that age, frequently earlier, they say they lose their suppleness and have to retire – at least from that particular dance.

A ceremony of almost Babylonian magnificence is a royal cremation. I was fortunate in seeing that of one of the three wives of the Raja of Bangli, together with five other corpses. Like almost everything in Bali, the occasion was one of great gaiety. In the village square were ranged six cremation lions, black with gilt manes, fierce eyes and crimson mouths. Overtopping every building in the neighbourhood were two cremation towers, highly ornate and multi-coloured, resting on bamboo frameworks for carrying.

The procedure started with 120 men lifting a tower and charging all over the square, zigzagging and shouting to mystify and frighten the evil spirits. The corpse was then brought out from the palace, where it had lain for five weeks in a mortuary – without refrigeration! – and deposited halfway up the tallest tower. The procession then moved off, men carrying lances and umbrellas in the lead, followed by women bearing offerings, four gamelan orchestras, the cremation lions, and, bringing up the rear, the towers. Very rightly, no-one looked sad during the whole performance, for everyone believed the spirit was released by this rite, and became a god.

On the cremation field funeral pyres had been built, and the corpse was brought down and placed inside a lion. Several groups of men made a pretence of fighting for the body, but no-one could really have wanted to get nearer to it than necessary. I soon discovered which way the wind was blowing, and tacked quickly up to windward. The lions stood underneath four-posted canopies above the two funeral pyres. The final rite was performed by a Brahmin priest, faggots were piled and the fires were lit. Flames and smoke leapt up, enveloping platform, lions, canopy and all. What happened to the charred remains I do not know. I had seen enough when small boys with long sticks were gleefully poking them through gaping holes in the sides of the lions.

Because of civil war in Indonesia, I had been almost the only European visitor in Bali. Perhaps I got a little tired of fending off vendors of souvenirs who had no other target. But I felt distressed that the calm dignity and friendly helpfulness natural to this quite unique people should give way to the undermining influences of commercialism. Alas, tourism has become one of Bali's main industries.

★   ★   ★

My feelings about sailing the Indian ocean are mixed. Whilst its 6,000 miles included the fastest long-distance passage of my whole voyage, it also treated me to the worst weather. The passage to the Cocos-Keeling Islands included four days of gale, during which the cockpit was a constant shower-bath. Things got wet below, and a sea came over when the hatch was open and flooded Stanley's bunk. On the other hand, our run between Cocos and Rodriguez was grand sailing. Covering the 2,000 miles in under fourteen days, we averaged 145 miles a day, and our best day's run was probably about 180 miles. Throughout the passage, *Solace* steered herself. We received friendly and generous hospitality at both groups of islands before going on to Mauritius, which was equally hospitable.

On September 26th we sailed out of Mauritius with a fine south-easterly breeze. I looked forward with interest to this leg of our journey: it would include the South African coast and the notorious Cape Agulhas, where there is no season of the year when the weather is good. It is a case of taking what comes, and it is bound to be nasty! The 4th and 5th October brought us hard blows. We were pooped more than once in heavy seas. Streaking along under twin staysails I was kept up all night, busy pumping, with an eye on the gear, but we were driving along in the right direction, and this continued to within two days of reaching the African coast. On the 10th the wind dropped to a flat calm. Albatrosses and petrels were flying around. I had a feeling that we were in for changed conditions. We certainly were.

At one o'clock in the morning the storm broke. The air was rent with thunder; sheet and forked lightning danced a devil's jig all round us. We lashed everything on deck. Rain followed, then a breeze got up, and by three-thirty was blowing a gale – from the south-west! We shut ourselves in down below and waited until it had blown itself out.

The following night was an unending succession of filthy black squalls and by daylight we had certainly had enough. The next five or six days were hard work, and after the next storm we were so tired that the alarm clock failed to rouse either of us, and waking at 2am I found that we had drifted across the shipping lane and ships were passing to seaward of us. The Agulhas current helped us a lot, and we passed the Cape of Good Hope on the 19th.

Our troubles were not over yet. The range running down from Table Mountain has an unpleasant reputation for 'williwaws' – sudden vicious squalls of wind which come rushing down the mountain-sides. Off Duiker Point, *Solace* danced a sort of highland fling for a couple of miles. Then – whoosh! Quickly down came the mizzen and over she leaned for the first williwaw. A further couple of miles of alternating calms and williwaws, then a patch of shifting light airs, then a steady breeze which carried us along to Table Bay, which to our disgust we found white with spume from a sou'-easter! This really seemed the last straw. Within a mile of the breakwater we started beating up against it, but were defeated. We ran down to Robin Island and anchored in the newly constructed boat-harbour to wait for the weather to moderate.

That wins the prize for the worst passage on the whole voyage.

Cape Town is celebrated – among yachtsmen at any rate – both for its hospitality and its wind. I knew well of the former, but had not heard of the latter. Bow and stern moorings were vacated so that *Solace* should lie in a secure berth close to the Royal Cape

Yacht Club. There she stayed for over a month while the sou'-easter did its best to blow her out to sea or the nor'-wester screamed in the opposite direction. One brought all the coal soot from the goods trains, the other brought the oil soot from the whaling fleet. Despite daily sweeping, it was impossible to keep the ship clean.

Having said that, everything else was on the credit side. I had been worried as to the sort of reception Stanley might get, and had made up my mind that as visitors we must conform to the local laws and conventions, but that if these should prove embarrassing we would continue on our way. In the event there was no comment, or even a hint of disapproval. The Yacht Club members were very friendly to Stanley. He was interviewed by a reporter from the 'coloured' newspaper, the *Golden City Post*, and felt he had really entered the hall of fame when he was able to say the next morning that he had 'been wrongly reported'!

On Friday, 12th December, we sailed for St Helena. Once clear of the African coast, we had a following wind for the whole way across the South Atlantic. From St Helena, with its fascinating Napoleonic associations and relics, we went on to Ascension Island, which is an astonishing place. There are forty volcanoes in its thirty-five or so square miles, but the mass of clinker and volcanic ash conceals in its centre an elevated oasis known as Green Mountain. Our Navy seems to have appreciated its possibilities, and the Marines, who took over the pioneering work, constructed batteries, roads, a pier, turtle ponds and, on Green Mountain, a farm and gardens. The garrison, of course, had to live on the foreshore, so two wells were sunk on Green Mountain, and pipes laid to carry water down to the troops. It was for this fresh water that we had put in, but we received a great deal more in terms of hospitality and interest. We then set off again for the West Indies, and Stanley's home.

Chapter 17

The weather was mild and pleasant and for eleven days we ran under twin staysails with a following breeze, I for the most part writing and typing, Stanley refitting, varnishing and studying. Stanley was one of the hardest workers I have ever known. It was in the matter of quality rather than quantity that he needed training, and by the time he left me his work by any standards would be considered first class.

When two people live at close quarters over long stretches of time, a very great deal of give and take is needed. Our temperaments were poles apart, though many of our tastes, especially those which mattered at sea, were similar. Our training could not have been more different – I with a somewhat Spartan upbringing and twenty-seven years in the Navy, Stanley a boy of under seventeen when he joined me, and of easy-going outlook. He needed a corkscrew to get him out of bed in the morning, and would probably admit that my cries of 'Heave ho, . . . Wakey wakey!' were the most unpleasant sounds of the day. On the other hand I, who prefer a quiet breakfast, had to put up with anything in the galley corner from 'Fight the Good Fight' to 'She's too Fat for Me.' The first four days of a passage I was spared these ordeals, as the vocalist was under the weather. Again, I like orderliness and tidiness – a place for everything and everything in its place. Stanley preferred to keep the contents of the fo'c'sle or the cockpit lockers scattered around on convenient little shelves in the cabin. My safely valve would periodically give a high pressure blast, and he would have a spring-clean.

Stanley was determined on a life at sea, and long cherished a hope of having a schooner in the West Indies which he would call the *Rosalind M, Mathurin*, after his mother. So I used to pull his leg and describe this vessel as I expected to find her one day – dirty paintwork, rusty rigging and so forth. One day he replied:

'What would you say if you saw my old schooner one day, no paint, frayed ropes, rusty wire, tattered sails – and *your* name on the bow and stern?'

In spite of my tantrums and irritability, Stanley was very loyal to me – more so than I deserved. I discovered that on several occasions, usually in a roundabout way. One day I made arrangements to meet a club member at 6.30pm at the Royal Cape Yacht Club. At 6.20 he arrived and was told by Stanley that I was in town.

'I arranged to meet Commander Clark here at six-thirty', said my host. 'Is he a punctual person?'

'Sir,' replied Stanley, according to my host, who was much impressed, 'Commander Clark is an officer of the Royal Navy, and if he said he would meet you at six-thirty he will do so.'

By a stroke of absolute luck I arrived at twenty-eight minutes past!

Stanley's mother was now working in British Guiana and had not seen him for over eight years. By the 8th February we were almost abreast the Demarara River, so I decided to side-step and put in there so that he could spend a week or so with her. Stanley was ashore as soon as we had found a safe berth at Georgetown, and was away up river for seventy miles to find his mother, whom he brought back to see the ship.

The night we sailed away, for the first time for nearly five years we sighted the Pole Star, in Latitude 8° north. Three days later we were heading for Kingstown light on St Vincent. In the Bequia Channel, *Solace* crossed her track of five years before, thus completing the circumnavigation an hour before midnight on 26th February 1959.

Some twelve days later, Stanley proudly sailed *Solace*, looking spick and span, up Castries harbour, tacking against a fresh breeze. He, too, had now circumnavigated the world. He had been preparing for the great day for months, and landed in his smartest attire. Subsequent to this, the *Voice of St Lucia* came out with a long article under prominent headlines: 'St Lucian First Coloured

Man to Sail Round World in Two-Man Boat'.

A day or two later he was looking a bit less cheerful.

'What's the matter, Stanley?'

'Oh-h, these people don't know anything. When they hear I've been round the world they ask me, "Have you been to America?" I say "No," and they ask, "Been to England?" – "No." "Been to Hong Kong?" – "No." "Tokyo?" – "No." "Singapore?" – "No." "Well, where the dickens have you been?" They've never heard of the places we've been to!'

★ ★ ★

At no time had I wanted publicity for my voyage, but getting wrecked on a Pacific Island, and on such an idyllic one as Palmerston, attracted the press in Britain and the Commonwealth at the time, and on my return I was approached with renewed interest by a number of newspapers as we made our landfall in Bantry Bay, Ireland. As my coffers were now completely empty, I gave a long interview to the *News Chronicle* for a six-day serial prior to my anticipated arrival at Plymouth, which duly appeared. I then spent some time cruising on the South Coast, before resuming life ashore with my long-suffering mother.

Mindful of Stanley's future, I wrote to the Vice Chairman of the Furness Withy Line, which operates in the West Indies, hoping to get him a job with them. The Vice Chairman replied that he did not consider that five and a half years experience in a yacht would be of any use to them. Eventually Stanley was accepted by the Henderson Line, in which he worked his way up to Mate and got his Master's ticket. He later tranferred to the Furness Withy Line, becoming Master of one of their ships, and I had the pleasure of writing to the above Vice Chairman (by then retired), sending him a copy of his 'refusal' letter of a few years previously and saying I was sure he would like to know that this young man was now Captain of one of his ships. I had no reply!

My summer of 1960 was very pleasantly occupied. The *News Chronicle* was sponsoring a new cabin cruiser – quite small – the prototype of which was named *Audacity*, and on its completion I was asked by the newspaper to take it on a publicity cruise, which would be fully reported by them, round Scotland. I had as crew one of the designer's sons and a *News Chronicle* photographer. I took her over on the Clyde and had several weeks' splendid sailing out to St Kilda, up to the Orkneys and Shetlands and down to Aberdeen.

I was also busy getting my book published, having had thirteen publishers on my tail on return from my voyage. I obtained excellent terms, and a well produced book resulted, with numerous pictures selected from the 1,500 or so transparencies taken on the voyage*. At the same time I started lecturing, the largest audience being for the Royal Geographical Society, which filled the Usher Hall in Edinburgh – over 3,000.

Over the succeeding years I gave some 250 lectures to every conceivable type of audience. Schools were particularly responsive, as one might expect, especially girls' schools. I always invited questions afterwards, and on one occasion a boy in the audience asked me if I was in the Boer War – which I hoped I might attribute to his historical ignorance rather than to my personal appearance.

My cruise in the *Audacity* included a visit to Kirkwall in Orkney, which coincided with a visit by the three-masted schooner *Prince Louis* from the Outward Bound Moray Sea School at Burghead and commanded by Commander Graham de Chair who, as Captain of the *Venus* had brought me home from Colombo in 1945. I went on board and was intrigued by the job she was doing. The following year I heard from Graham that he needed a relief skipper for a cruise in the late autumn, so I took the job for a month or so. Shortly afterwards Graham decided to retire and I was asked by Admiral Dunbar-Nasmith, who was on the Committee, if I would take over as skipper permanently. After some hesitation I accepted, and took her over in the spring of 1962.

Four enjoyable and very worth while years followed. The Sea School Warden was Major Pat Steptoe and the Chief Instructor

On the Wind of a Dream, published by Hutchinson.

was Tony Montgomery, who ran the mountain expeditions and organised the course generally, whilst I ran the seamanship as well as the ship, the main items of seamanship equipment being four dipping lug cutters. The four of us worked in complete harmony. About a hundred young men between the ages of sixteen and twenty came for a month at the School, there being nine courses a year, as well as one Senior course for adults.

The *Prince Louis* could only accommodate twenty-four, so she had to do four cruises, each of three days or so, late in the course, so that the crew had time to acquire the elementary seamanship knowledge needed. Cruises included Scapa Flow in Orkney, Cromarty Firth, Inverness Firth and sometimes through the Pentland Firth to Loch Eriboll and places on the West Coast such as the Sound of Mull, where we met the cutters which had come through the Caledonian Canal, and changed over crews with them.

Passing through Pentland Firth depended to some extent on weather conditions. On a west-going tide with a strong westerly wind, overfalls at the Merry Men of May could be so dangerous that, according to the Admiralty Pilot, a schooner or small steamer might never be heard of again! – a caution which I always read to the trainees to give them a bit of excitement. Scapa Flow was my favourite training ground, as it is completely land-locked, is a good five miles across, and I could lower the ship's boats in weather which would have rendered it impossible outside. It also had a number of anchorages which afforded shelter in any direction of wind. Then, too, there were the historical associations with the wreck of the *Royal Oak*, and those remaining of the German High Seas Fleet which scuttled itself in 1919. For a run ashore there was the quaint little town of Stromness, or the island of Hoy where the Hope Ness lifeboat was based.

It was at Burghead that I first met Dr Kurt Hahn, ex-Headmaster of Gordonstoun and founder of Outward Bound. We soon became friends, as he was firmly of the opinion that the *Prince Louis* was the best thing in Outward Bound. It was a disaster for the Moray Sea School when, as the result of a fatal accident on an expedition in the Cairngorms, both Pat Steptoe and

Tony Montgomery were most unwisely relieved of their responsibilities. No-one of anything like their calibre ever succeeded them.

The new Warden disliked the *Prince Louis*, regarding it correctly as an empire within his empire, since he was quite unqualified to interfere with its activities, and he made up his mind to get rid of it. It had always been expensive to run, and the other Outward Bound schools had always resented the extra drain on funds, so it was not all that difficult to get the School Committee to decide in 1966 that the ship must be sold. When the decision was taken I wired to Kurt Hahn in Germany, and he was over in a flash, very angry; but he failed to get the decision altered.

Chapter 18

An idea had meanwhile matured in my mind, that I could run the *Prince Louis* as a seagoing school, quite independent of a shore base, with just an administrative office for recruiting, etc. This was fully discussed with Lt Comdr Patrick Job, who lived at Plockton on the West Coast and had been to sea with me a number of times. His opinion was that if he ran the administration from his house at Plockton, and the ship had a mooring there, the scheme was perfectly feasible.

The problem of finance was likely to be difficult, so Kurt Hahn took me to Buckingham Palace for a forty-minute interview with Prince Philip, his old pupil, in the course of which I had to explain my methods and, as tactfully as possible, why they were much superior to those of the Sail Training Association which he supported! He agreed to give it his backing and persuaded Lord Dulverton and Sir James Miller to finance experimental cruises. Kurt Hahn and I went to see Lord Dulverton at Loch Eil in Scotland, and he expressed great interest in the cruises and promised his support. I then paid a courtesy call on Sir James Miller in his Edinburgh office, to explain my plans.

I had scarcely opened my mouth before Sir James, who was a keen supporter of the STA, started to tell me how I was to run the ship!

'I wish', he said, leaning back in his chair with half closed eyes and hands folded upon his ample tummy, 'I wish the ship to be based on Glasgow; I wish it to be run like the STA, with courses of a fortnight' – and so on.

I felt it necessary to interrupt him quickly, so I said 'I'm sorry, Sir James, but I am not prepared to run the ship on those lines.'

I do not think he had ever been spoken to like that before and there was a pause of at least a minute before he said, 'Well, Commander, it may take me a little time to find another skipper.'

I played my trump card. 'I must remind you, Sir James, that Lord Dulverton is also financing these cruises and is in entire agreement with my plans, which also have the approval of Prince Philip, to whom I have explained them.'

A long silence followed, then, 'Well, Commander, I will continue to support the scheme but I shall not serve on the Committee.'

I was particularly relieved to hear the latter. Sir James was as good as his word – and in view of the royal approval could hardly have been otherwise.

The net result was that I was able to carry out mixed sailing and mountaineering courses throughout the autumn as a pilot scheme, with a view to a bigger ship later on. These courses were an unqualified success and Kurt Hahn strongly supported our view that a successor to the *Prince Louis* should be sought which would accommodate thirty-six trainees and so be financially viable. Lord Dulverton was convinced that the scheme should continue with a bigger ship and I was told to look for one.

I went to Norway, then to Portugal, where I found an ex-Grand Banks fishing schooner, in superb condition, capable of being converted to square rig and big enough to contain everything I wanted – the *Hortense*, priced at £18,000. I estimated that she could be converted for another £40,000. My committee was unable to approve purchase because of one dissident member. After a time he was convinced and I was told to arrange purchase. Two days later we were told that *Hortense* had been removed from the sales list, to be preserved as a national memorial and harbour training ship for young fishermen! So the search started again, until Lord Dulverton said we had tried hard enough and he would have a ship built to my requirements. Kurt Hahn and I were on air!

My requirements were given to a well known yacht designer, who became so awkward and argumentative that we decided to take it out of his hands and leave it to the ship builder, John Mackenzie of Herd and Mackenzie, Buckie, to build on the uncompleted plans, modified to my requirements. The firm made a superb job of it and in due course the ship was launched by Lady Jane Nelson, an impressive service being carried out by the Moderator of the General Assembly of the Church of Scotland and my brother Gordon. The ship was ready for the first cruise in October 1971, being based at Plockton.

The name *Captain Scott* was given to her after one diehard Scot had written to the paper, furious that a ship built in Scotland and due to operate in Scottish waters, and doubtless with a large proportion of Scottish trainees, should be named after 'that English pirate', Sir Francis Drake!

The four-week training schedule consisted of a week's training on board, either at anchor or under way, followed by a week-end walking and camping expedition ashore, another week's sailing, a second week-end expedition in the mountains, a third week sailing, a third mountain expedition and a final week cruising under sail, all instruction for sea and land being carried out on board by a fully qualified permanent staff, supplemented by one temporary seamanship instructor and two temporary mountaineers. As far as training went, the ship was entirely self-contained. The alternation of sea and land activities worked splendidly and ensured that trainees never got bored. After a few days training on board they were ready to stretch their legs ashore, but by the end of the expedition they were glad to be back on board.

Cruising was mainly in the coastal area between Orkney and the Clyde, its numerous sheltered anchorages and magnificent mountain scenery providing the perfect elements for our particular scheme. St Kilda was at the western extremity, and Shetland and the Isle of Man were the northern and southern limits. One expedition was carried out in the Lake District from Whitehaven, otherwise we never went south of the North Channel, as the coast to the north of it was so admirably suited to our requirements.

Among our favourite anchorages was Loch Shieldaig in Loch Torridon, where we had two hospitable friends who entertained us when changing over crews with the mountaineers. We became well known to all the villagers, who got a shock one day when the ship entered harbour with a 'man' hanging from the yardarm! They were convinced that the crew had mutinied and that it was I who was hanging there! In fact it was a hammock inside an oilskin jacket and trousers, a pair of seaboots tied on the bottom, with my sou'wester strapped on top of a ball coir fender, and when strung aloft it looked for all the world like a man with a broken neck.

Our clientele was a complete cross-section of British youth, from public school to Borstal, with a sprinkling from overseas. In the course of three years we had trainees from seventeen countries, from America to Tibet.

Of particular interest on one course, were some Borstal boys sent by an altruistic Scottish gentleman. I had expected two, but there were three – two brothers and a close friend. Their benefactor had explained to them that the course was tough and they had agreed to go through with it. On the very first evening the Mate informed me that they wanted to go home. I sent for them in my cabin, where they stood looking down at their toes whilst I questioned them, getting no reply except 'Don't like them. Want to go home.' They felt different from the others.

I told them they were to keep their bargain with their benefactor and stay. We moved round from Plockton to an anchorage in Loch Alsh for the first night and in the morning it became clear to both the Mate and me that the three intended to desert when the ship went alongside the jetty at Kyle for fresh water and provisions. I had already seen enough of them on deck to realise that they had plenty of spirit and in my judgement would do well if only I could hold on to them for the first three days or so. So instead of going alongside at Kyle, to their chagrin I anchored off and sent a boat inshore for provisions, deciding to postpone watering for a couple of days when we should be in Stornaway.

We then anchored in Broadford Bay, outside what I judged to be swimming distance, for sail drills, the three Borstal Boys being given stations aloft on the yards. They obviously enjoyed it, as I had expected. The next day we sailed for Stornaway with a spanking breeze on our quarter up the Minch, ideal for sail training. Our normal routine on anchoring at Stornaway was to send the boys on a three-mile run, giving them twenty minutes in the town afterwards before returning on board. So there was every chance of escape, and the Mate suggested that the Borstal boys should be kept on board; but I judged that they were 'hooked' on the ship by now, so they were allowed ashore – and all three returned afterwards.

We then sailed for Galloway in the Shetlands for the first expedition. One of the three caught a chill in the hills and had to go to Lerwick hospital. When the staff there told him they would be keeping him there overnight, his reply, significantly, was, 'No, I want to go *home* to the ship.' We had no further doubts about them and they completed an excellent course, after which they all got jobs with the Forestry Commission. Their sponsor was so pleased that he said he would be sending another fifteen, but the Social Services were less enlightened, and did not send them.

An incentive to good language and behaviour on the messdeck was the girl cook – the only female on board – on whom I had insisted for psychological reasons against the wishes of my Committee. Her galley was just above the trainees' messdeck, and within earshot. Events more than justified my insistence; moreover it had amusing results. I had an occasional press reporter interviewing me, and as soon as I mentioned that we had a girl cook on board – and a pretty blonde at that – he would be out of my cabin like a shot and off to the galley. Two thirds of the resulting article would be devoted to Margot, with a photo! Both Margot and, when she got married, her successor Anna, were a great success. All our three girl cooks got married, one to a fisherman and the other two to our bosun and our engineer!

I ran the *Captain Scott* for exactly three years (1971-1974) after watching her being built. I handed her over to my relief skipper (whom I was allowed by Lord Dulverton to choose) on getting engaged to be married – swallowing the anchor, so to speak, and acquiring a ball and chain! The ship continued to run from Loch Eil for another year under my successor, and was then sold to the Sultan of Oman. The Sultan enquired whether I would go out there and run her on the same lines. However, I had become engaged to my future wife and was firmly of the opinion that the job was one for a completely dedicated batchelor, so I declined.

A tragic event marred the four-year record. One of the trainees, a fine young man who was a splendid swimmer and a high diver, asked for permission to dive from the lower yard, which I approved. He then repeated it perfectly from the topsail yard. I then approved his request to dive from the topgallant yard, of which he appeared quite confident. He misjudged his 'take-off' and at the bottom of the 80-foot dive came a belly-flopper. Going down to the bottom, probably unconscious, he was drowned before his condition was realised and we were able to dive in and pull him up. It was particularly sad for me that this had happened on the last day of my last cruise. There had been no serious accident previous to this in four years.

On retiring as skipper of the *Captain Scott* I renewed an old contact with Basil Clarkson's Viking Cruises on the Norfolk Broads, with which I had helped him for several years after the War, either as Skipper of one of the eleven yachts or as Commodore of the Fleet. Each boat carried five or six public school boys and a Skipper and Mate. After early morning inspection each day we sailed until late afternoon, mooring up at some suitable bank with a background of reeds and all gathering for a meeting in an enormous balloon tent. Towards the end of the week there would be a yacht race for the skippers and a dinghy race for the boys. 'Shooting' Ludham Bridge was one of the excitements. Mast and sails had to be lowered to get under the bridge. A well drilled crew would do a crash 'down mast and sails', relying on the boat's way to carry it under the bridge, then 'up mast and sails' on the far side. Those who had not the skill and nerve would make fast to the bank, and lower before quanting through, and the same on the far side before re-hoisting. The evening meetings were of a very definite Christian content.

Not long after the War, I came in contact with Moral Re-Armament and paid a ten-day visit to its centre at Caux in Switzerland – to the dismay of some relatives and friends – after having been to its London headquarters many times and worked

127

with its teams. I was tremendously impressed and utterly convinced of its soundness, and remember wiring to my sceptical brother, 'This is the Kingdom of God on the march.' I later paid another visit to Caux, a third one with my mother and some years later a fourth one with my wife.

★ ★ ★

It was in 1973, at the Autumn Conference of the Officers' Christian Union, that I had met the young lady who eventually became my wife. I mentioned my interest to a mutual acquaintance, Captain Godfrey Buxton, who said 'That's good! She's a fine young Christian. Her father is a Brigadier living in Surrey. Would you like me to have a dinner party for you and her – or perhaps it would be less obvious if others were invited too.' That did not seem right to me, as I understood that she farmed with her parents and brother in Somerset. On querying this with Godfrey he replied, 'I'm so sorry, Victor, you are quite right. I was thinking of her cousin.' (The cousin was in her mid-twenties and married!) He added 'That's a bit too far for a dinner party, so why not invite yourself down to help on their farm?'

I thought that an excellent suggestion, so I did – only to get a cool reply that the house would be full for some time with visitors. Not to be put off, I suggested a visit in the spring. This seemed to suit the family and in the event I spent the whole summer farming with them – and pursuing my main objective!

Danae tells me that I never did propose but took things for granted, and we were married at Dunster on May 10th 1975. We now have two daughters, Jessica and Rosalind. A friend who knew all about my previous adventurous life wrote to me 'Well, Victor, you've had it all ways.' Which was not far from the truth.